Global Governance

Key Concepts series

GLOBAL GOVERNANCE

Timothy J. Sinclair

polity

The right of Timothy J. Sinclair to be identified as Author of this Work
has been asserted in accordance with the UK Copyright, Designs and
Patents Act 1988.

First published in 2012 by Polity Press

Polity Press
65 Bridge Street
Cambridge CB2 1UR, UK

Polity Press
350 Main Street
Malden, MA 02148, USA

ISBN-13: 978-0-7456-3529-3
ISBN-13: 978-0-7456-3530-9 (pb)

A catalogue record for this book is available from the British Library.

Typeset in 10.5 on 12 pt Sabon
by Toppan Best-set Premedia Limited
Printed and bound in Great Britain by the MPG Books Group

The publisher has used its best endeavours to ensure that the URLs for
external websites referred to in this book are correct and active at the
time of going to press. However, the publisher has no responsibility for
the websites and can make no guarantee that a site will remain live or
that the content is or will remain appropriate.

Every effort has been made to trace all copyright holders, but if any have
been inadvertently overlooked the publisher will be pleased to include
any necessary credits in any subsequent reprint or edition.

For further information on Polity, visit our website:
www.politybooks.com

To Uncle Jack and Nigel

Contents

Acknowledgements

In thinking about how to organize my thoughts I have found inspiration in the work of Niall Ferguson and especially Partha Dasgupta. I would like to thank Shirin Rai for her interest in this book, and Hazel Smith for her encouragement. Martin Hewson is to blame for getting me thinking about global governance in the first place. Rorden Wilkinson gave me valuable advice and some thoughtful insights at a crucial moment. Some of the ideas in this volume have been discussed with audiences at the University of Delaware, the University of Auckland, the Victoria University of Wellington and the University of York. I am most appreciative of the questions and comments provided by these audiences.

At Polity, I have been greatly aided by Dr Louise Knight, Rachel Donnelly, Emma Hutchinson and David Winters. Working with Polity has been a pleasure throughout. Thanks are also due to the anonymous reviewers for Polity, who helped me improve the manuscript.

My spouse, Nicole Lindstrom, has been a source of support and guidance throughout this project. In particular, she greatly assisted with some of the ideas in chapter 4.

John Norris (Jack) Cox (1925–2005) and his son Nigel (1951–2006), my uncle and cousin respectively, were thoughtful, resourceful, creative men. Jack, a skilled educator and civil servant, helped build the institutions of post-war New

Zealand society. His son, Nigel, the writer, did what writers do, with growing confidence, to increasing acclaim. This book is dedicated to their memory.

Timothy J. Sinclair
Stoneleigh Abbey, Warwickshire, 9 January 2012

1
Introduction

What is global governance and what might it be? Global governance is a challenge to the way our world has been managed since the emergence of nation-states in seventeenth-century Europe. Most of us think of states making decisions independently but global governance implies the need to make decisions collectively, given the rise of common problems like global warming and terrorism. At the most basic level then, global governance implies change in what states are and what they can do as new ways of making decisions and acting on collective problems develop. But global governance, like states, can develop in different ways. Some states are tyrannical, and allow little freedom of expression to their communities, while others allow for free speech and democracy. Global governance can develop along multilateral and democratic lines, or it too could devolve into a more dictatorial or autocratic form. This is why knowing about how people think about global governance is so important.

Global governance is a difficult idea to get away from these days. As a concept, global governance seems to capture something very important about our world in the second decade of the twenty-first century. It represents a yearning of some sort, but whether that yearning is for peace and justice, or mere maintenance of the status-quo order, is less clear. Anxiety about global uncertainty seems important (Wilkinson 2005a: 1–3). In these circumstances, most of us tend to ask about the essence of global governance. What does the concept really mean, and why is it important? This book will tackle these questions, not by telling you what I think is the correct approach to global governance, but by investigating how people think about global governance in different ways, the dimensions and implications of the views they hold, and where applicable, the more systematic thinking we might identify as theories which try to make sense of a complex world.

When Non-Governmental Organizations (NGOs) talk about the need for the international community to review what went on in the Sri Lankan civil war, when consumers complain about high oil prices and the rising costs of food and clothing, and when states debate military action against regimes, we can be sure that the idea of global governance will be invoked. Unfortunately, the substance of global governance is often far from clear. For some users of the term it means unified action against specific threats; for others, merely a framework of rules and norms. Other groups equate global governance with tyranny or a conspiracy to establish world government. This book investigates these ideas.

Global governance is not just an academic debate, as interesting as that can be. The implications of global governance affect us all. In order to illustrate this I have created two fictional families, one living in the US and the other in India. In chapters 3 to 8, these families adopt the perspective on global governance considered in each chapter. My hope is that you will obtain a more concrete understanding of what each idea of global governance might actually mean through these fictional vignettes, as family life meets different conceptions of global political organization. Studies of international relations too often neglect the probable implications of the phenomena they address, making these things seem distant and abstract. It is especially important to bring the global down to the local with global governance because, as with pollution and gender, it often has quite specific implications for everyday life, and is not confined just to the level of state–state interaction.

The prototypical American Mason family of Greenport, New York had not, until recently, discussed international issues, never mind this thing called global governance. They were not a politically minded household. Normally, they were happy to leave policy, and especially foreign policy, to politicians in Washington. But John, the husband and father, had recently become concerned about coastal erosion close to the winery he manages on the north fork of Long Island, near Shelter Island. The beautiful, historic north fork of Long Island contains settlements as old as colonial America. How startling in this land of the big and the new to come across police cars carrying town seals proclaiming foundation dates in the seventeenth century. John was finding he had to work much harder to keep ahead of climate change. Thinking about new varieties of grapes in this context was a challenging job. What if the region and its extensive vineyards prove vulnerable to the changing weather? What will happen to the businesses that have grown in the local soil?

The Mason children – Henry, sixteen, and Sofia, fourteen – are worried too. They are still in high school, but can see that things are going to be different for them. Obsessed by environmental issues, they are both becoming advocates of change in the way things are done in the household. Henry wants to design eco-friendly houses. Sofia is interested in clothing recycling. All this is a very great distance from John and his wife Helen's own teenage obsessions with V8s and the local mall. The children are not afraid – as children aren't – to make it clear to their parents that the old ways of thinking and acting are no longer acceptable.

John's wife Helen, too, is getting worried. Her concerns include traffic congestion in what had once been an idyllic refuge from the problems of urban America. She also worries about energy supplies and, increasingly, about carbon emissions. Now, more and more, dinner-table conversation ranges further than the standard talk with the kids about where they are going on vacation next summer. What could be done about these problems, they wonder, and who is going to fix them?

The Patel family lives thousands of miles away from the Masons, and in very different conditions. For them, home is Bangalore (or Bengaluru), capital of the state of Karnataka in south India. Bangalore, the third largest city in India after Mumbai and Delhi, is often known as the Garden City. The Patels moved to the city from the countryside seven years ago.

The Patels are not poor by Indian standards. Nor are they rich. One of the sources of anxiety for Agastya, the husband and father, and Bhadraa, his wife, is the fear that they will get sick and fall into poverty. Coming to Bangalore is part of their effort to get away from these fears and participate in the high-growth India, the 'India Shining' the media talks so much about. Agastya runs a small cleaning business, servicing some of the software companies in Bangalore that have led the city to be known as the Silicon Valley of India. The Patels have four children: Aditi, fourteen; Vinod, thirteen; and the twins Janna and Mira, ten. Mr and Mrs Patel have high hopes for the prosperity and security of their children.

Environmental issues do not have the same prominence in family conversation amongst the Patels as they do in the Masons' household. The senior Patels are more interested in India becoming a rich country as quickly as possible, and in their children working hard, passing their examinations with good grades and securing well-paying jobs in expanding companies. They do not want their children to work in the family cleaning business. Although generally positive toward the West, the family, like many citizens of emerging market countries, are concerned by any effort to put a brake on economic growth, thinking it unfair for the West to obstruct development in India out of concern for the global ecosystem. The Patel children, although more circumspect about it than the Masons', do not always share these parental views. They have been more influenced by television and the internet, and are aware that their environment is not as clean as in other countries. Aditi and Vinod wonder whether part of getting rich is cleaning up the filth that has been a normal part of urban India in the past.

These two families, although facing many of the same problems of life, are very different from each other in important ways. For the Masons, many of the basic functions of the household are unproblematic. Water is safe to drink; waste is effectively removed via the public sewer system; although public transport is very poor where they live, the roads are good and they have two large and relatively new automobiles. Although the Patels are relatively prosperous by Indian standards, many of the things the Masons take for granted are a problem for them. Electricity supply is intermittent, the sewers flood in the monsoon season, and Bangalore is a crowded place. In thinking about these families and their views, we must keep in mind the inequalities between them. We can expect this, and the history of these inequalities, to shape their thinking, giving rise to different ideas. Although the Patels and Masons can think for themselves, they do face different circumstances with different resources and opportunities at their disposal.

The problem of global governance

The apocryphal Mason and Patel families are hardly unique. Everywhere around the world, in rich neighbourhoods and in the desperately poor, people often reach toward an understanding of problems that cross borders and whose solution will require more than the usual national policy choices by governments acting in isolation from each other. Although this is inevitably a process dominated by the educated elite, broader opinion can influence political choices, as the Arab spring of 2011 showed. This pervasive sense of the interconnectedness of the world, and therefore of the necessity for global solutions to problems, seems significant. It may be the best hope for the human race. This makes the idea of global governance important, exciting and worthy of close study. Close study must include not just speculating about the world we want, but careful examination of the world we have, including the ways of thinking that shape it. The choices made by states, peoples and individuals are crucially shaped by ideas about the world held as axioms, or taken-for-granted assumptions, by others. Collectively held ideas are enormously powerful. The state, for example, is not really a collection of guns, soldiers and buildings. The state, first and foremost, is a collectively held idea that the government is legitimate. When that idea breaks down, the state is in trouble, as seen in Tunisia, Egypt and Libya. Collectively held ideas are not immutable. They change. We must keep in mind that in other eras, such as the twenty years or so prior to the First World War, many people in the rich countries shared a similar sense that the world was coming together in positive ways.

More than thirty years later, after two wars which destroyed tens of millions of lives, the scope for peaceful cooperation was less self-evident.

Although there may be some implicit agreement on the problems associated with these challenges, there is very little agreement on how to deal with them. Global governance, although a term often used by educated people, is typically deployed without clarity, like references to the 'good life' or 'human progress'. For some users, global governance is nothing more than a contemporary way to refer to international institutions. For these authors, there is nothing new in global governance and the term has no specific content, even though they are happy to adopt the new language. For others, global governance implies a change in the fundamental political units that rule our world, incorporating new forms of authority that recognize the technical complexity of a world characterized by economic integration (Rosenau 1992). Some thinkers see the potential for expanding democracy in this new emphasis on global governance, undermining established elites and traditions of inequality, while others see the perpetuation of elite control in a story about continuity (Dryzek 2010; Higgott and Erman 2010). Still others reject the very idea of global governance, seeing in it a sinister plot to undermine their state and national autonomy.

Before we can be effective advocates of global governance, if that is our objective, it is essential to clarify the range of thinking about what I will call the problem of global governance. This requires we put aside the idea that it is an agreed notion, self-evident to all, and come to grips with the diversity of thinking about the idea. By casting global governance as a problem, I wish to reinforce the understanding that the objectives of global governance and the means of achieving these objectives are not collectively held ideas in the same way as notions of the state.

Approach

This book examines these competing concepts of global governance, describing them, analysing them and evaluating them. Among the elements covered are key puzzles, actors, assumptions, implications and, prior to the scenarios, strengths, weaknesses and likely future development. I have avoided long literature reviews. Toward the end of each substantive chapter, I have incorporated some special analysis. In the tradition of counterfactual analysis in the social sciences, which encourages us to imagine alternative realities if prior conditions were different, each of the substantive chapters uses scenarios or historical vignettes in which the Patels and Masons adopt the broad outline assumptions of each perspective on global governance, conditioned by their different circumstances, as presented in successive chapters, as a way to bring home the meaning and significance of each view of global governance (Ferguson 1999: 1–90; Sinclair 2005: 16). These scenarios focus upon the global financial crisis that started in 2007, climate change, development, security and gender relations.

The book should provide the reader with an introduction to a range of different understandings of global governance. It needs to be said that some ways of thinking about world politics are greatly concerned with global governance. In other approaches, references to global governance are more implicit. One way of organizing this book would have been to focus only on those approaches that talk about global governance and to ignore the others. But this would produce a rather unrepresentative book that ignores the range of views. It is that range that seems particularly valuable in a book of this nature. The range of ideas presented in chapters 3 to 7 undermines claims of any particular approach, or any special class of actors, to a monopoly over the definition of global governance. I am not presenting a positive or normative account of concepts of global governance. I assume no approach to global governance is self-evidently the right one and that it is ultimately up to the reader to decide, based on a reasoned examination, which approach or approaches might be cogent and for what purposes.

This is not a book that seeks to describe or provide a typology of empirical global governance institutions or processes in exhaustive detail. For one thing, given the different views of what global governance comprises found in this book, a representative empirical treatment would go well beyond a discussion of international organizations. My objective is to treat global governance as the problem, rather than assume we know what global governance is, and move on to understanding how it works. You will not find within these pages lengthy descriptions of international regimes, institutions or private authorities. Those things can be found elsewhere, as in Karns and Mingst (2009), Hewson (2005) and Drezner (2007: 71–85). A focus on empirical material of this sort would undermine my central concern with competing ways of thinking about global governance and the significance of each approach. That is the purpose of this volume. I have also excluded explicit focus on international law in this book, as this is a separate and fascinating study (Reus-Smit 2004). Many examples and scenarios involving the Masons and Patels have been included in this book to ground the competing conceptualizations in a relevant and interesting way. I have specifically avoided any substantial consideration of the public policy debates about *governance* (Kjaer 2004), reasoning that global governance is a different and complementary literature and therefore worthy of analysis on its own terms. I have incorporated the academic debate about global governance, such as it is, into this book, as it links with the perspectives considered. A handful of complementary volumes published by others provide longer excerpts and specially written chapters that are useful reading in conjunction with this volume (Hewson and Sinclair 1999; Wilkinson 2005b; Whitman 2009; Diehl and Frederking 2010).

Argument

A specific argument organizes the analysis in this book. Although, as we will see, diverse approaches to thinking about world politics take a view on global governance, or enable a view to be inferred, in terms of both what global governance is and what objectives global governance should have, the impetus behind the debate about global governance has its origins in the policy world. Global governance here represents a quite limited managerial view of the world. This is in large part a reaction to the failure of prior programmes for global change, as argued in chapter 2. These managerial underpinnings serve to limit the concept of global governance and undermine analysis of the concept's broader political implications. The managerial origins of global governance do not prevent more radical perspectives from offering alternative views. But they do tend to undermine the claims of these other views.

Global life, if we can call it that, increasingly throws up seemingly novel and challenging institutions, processes and relationships. Some of this we have come to label 'globalization'. However, how we understand this change today and how we respond to it shares much with how we responded to the advent of the gold standard regime or the Bretton Woods system following World War II. Global governance, while a recognition of new phenomena, is not, as a way of thinking, so very new itself (Hewson 2008: 1). It remains a limited and partial concept, rather than system-changing.

Contrary to much of the excitement about global governance then, the substantive story about this concept is one of continuity rather than novelty. It is the new language in which our policy-makers and scholars have learnt to debate the nature of the world's problems since the mid-1990s. So, although change is not the main focus of this story, it is an important story. Most broadly, what is really interesting about global governance is the terrain it provides for a debate about how to deal with those of the world's problems that cannot be limited to national governments. In this sense, chapters 3 to 8 represent different tendencies in a contest about the approach that will dominate policy in the years to come.

Plan of this book

The debate about global governance is complex and multi-faceted. I have tried to cut through this to what I consider the most important elements, although no doubt other authors would make different judgements. In order to establish a sound foundation for these substantive chapters, I have provided a reading of the historical origins of the debate about global governance in chapter 2. This is an important chapter because it quickly becomes clear just how much continuity is really central to the story about global governance. This chapter should be read before the substantive chapters. Chapters 3 to 8 address, respectively, what I label 'Institutionalism' (chapter 3), 'Transnationalism' (chapter 4), 'Cosmopolitanism' (chapter 5), 'Hegemonism' (chapter 6), 'Feminism' (chapter 7) and 'Rejectionism' (chapter 8).

In each chapter I have extrapolated the implications of this way of thinking, as well as its sense of what matters and what does not. I evaluate strengths and weaknesses and try to provide some sense of the future development of the concept. I try to do this explication in as systematic and methodical a way as possible within the limits of short chapters. The hypothetical vignettes involving the Mason and Patel families help illustrate the differences in views and the concrete implications of these differences. Concreteness, in the context of a debate about ideas, is advantageous to understanding. I have chosen to focus on interesting topical problems most of us will have some familiarity with: the global financial crisis that began in 2007; climate change; development; security; and gender relations. This element of each chapter will have more of a narrative quality to it than the rest. I incorporate the Mason and Patel families in a less systematic way in the following chapter. Global governance is usually debated in quite abstract terms, and some of that will be evident here too. But global governance is very much a problem of concern to us all as citizens of the world. Making the problem of global governance relevant and compelling is essential.

2
Emergence

Sorting out how people think about global governance is a challenge. Specific concepts and broader frameworks of thought develop and change over time in both the policy and academic worlds. Ideas that are prevalent at one time may reflect a specific understanding of how certain problems are effectively addressed. When the problem or issue changes, the concept or framework might be abandoned, developed further or transformed entirely. Intellectual changes themselves can also drive forward new ways of thinking about old problems, so that issues we may have thought of as intractable suddenly seem subject to improvement. In the human or social world, change often occurs simultaneously in circumstances and in our ways of thinking, making understanding doubly difficult. Compounding all of this is the reality that different and competing understandings cloud any unitary comprehension of the concept. Given the potential for complexity, it would not be surprising if the Masons and Patels found these debates confusing and frustrating.

In thinking about ideas and their success in influencing policy we need to distinguish between a rationalist understanding of this process and one based on social construction. Rationalism assumes ideas are selected for their merits and judged on their successes. Such an approach has difficulty with the persistence of ideas when their success has been strongly questioned, such as Nazism after 1943 and Soviet

Communism from around 1970 onwards. The persistence of these ideas despite their lack of effectiveness suggests that other than purely rational aggregation of interests is at stake. It may be, of course, that small elite groups benefited from Nazism and Soviet Communism despite their declining fortunes. Or it may be that other than rational factors were involved. Constructivist theories suggest that collectively held ideas, norms and assumptions, such as the legitimacy of the state (in most rich countries), are consequential (Bjola and Kornprobst 2010). Although not physical entities, ideas can be so widely held that they shape human behaviour as if they are material facts like rivers or volcanoes. These social facts (Searle 2005) become like a play book, conditioning our thoughts and actions, until major events like depression, war and revolution give rise to the possibility of their transformation. A useful way to think about the debate over global governance is that it involves trying to rewrite the play book to get the favoured ideas enshrined in our habits, norms and expectations. So the debate is not about the finer points of academic understanding, but about getting the broad framework of ideas accepted so that they are consequential and taken for granted in our daily lives.

If we think about our prototypical families for a moment, the significance of this should be clear. The Patels and Masons think about what they do, and they are aware of what others do too. Implicit in this are expectations or intersubjectively held assumptions about the world that the Patels and Masons regard as rules. These rules, which for the Patels and Masons are just as real or material as a physical thing, guide their behaviour and shape what they tell their political leaders individually and collectively. These rules are not unchanging, but when they are established they can be hard to change even in the face of great challenges. The consequences of the establishment of these frameworks are great and so it is no wonder that the debates that surround them can be so ferocious and that participants can be so tenacious in pursuing them. Rather than some purely academic debate, these are the stakes that underpin the conflict between competing conceptions of global governance.

Global governance is a relatively recent and increasingly widely used concept. As I suggested in the introduction to this book, as with some other concepts, there is considerable debate about what global governance is, the purpose of the concept and the broader thinking associated with it. In this chapter, I attempt to sort out some of this confusion by giving you an overview of the origins of the debate about the concept and how it has been applied in concrete situations. The discussion starts with 'international organization', the concept which served as a precursor to global governance.

International organization as organizing principle

Two ideas about how to manage international relations competed at the end of World War II. For many in the academic community and amongst the political establishment in the Allied nations, the devastation of the Great War, as it was then known, and World War II seemed to show the folly of the idealism that first became popular in the 1920s. Idealist thought suggested that cooperation between states was possible, and that misunderstanding and misperception were the reasons why cooperation failed, leading to military conflict. What was necessary for idealists was the creation of institutions in which state representatives could meet so that grievances could be expressed, perceptions clarified and problems resolved.

Against this idealism, a new 'Realism', as it came to be known, became a widely held view of international relations after World War II. In the Realist worldview, states are driven to pursue their advantage at the cost of other states. The world is a zero-sum game, the Realists suggested, in which some states win and others lose. For Realists, the key issue in international relations is therefore the relative advantage enjoyed by any state in comparison to other states. This advantage could be acquired by unilateral action and, where appropriate, tough negotiation. As popularly depicted in the movie *Fail Safe*, Realists thought human nature typically did not allow for another way of behaving. Realists thought the Liberal–Idealist views championed by US President Woodrow Wilson and the League of Nations had been proven wrong by the renewal of great-power war, and may have even encouraged the outbreak of conflict in the 1930s.

Curiously, the popularity of the Realist view, reinforced by half a decade of war and many years of severe economic difficulties between the wars, did not stop the victorious Allies from establishing the body we know as the United Nations, in October 1945. Unlike the League of Nations, the UN was conceived as an active peace-maker. Indeed, the Allies used the term 'United Nations' from early in 1942 to designate their military alliance against German and Japanese military power. After World War II, UN forces again undertook a peace-making role fighting in the Korean peninsula.

The UN enjoyed prestige as an effective institution in the 1940s and 1950s. This was a time of gathering tension between the East and West – the onset of the Cold War – and the United Nations was a key place in which elements of this tension were managed, where the high politics of peace and security could be addressed in practical ways. It was during this time that the idea of international organization came firmly into focus in academic and policy-making circles. International organization, although never explicitly articulated officially, was nevertheless an ambitious concept that suggested most problems between states were not about survival (Claude 1971: 6). International organization implied a 'continuing partnership' beyond the war to share 'knowledge, resources, and responsibility in the effort to create a peaceful and stable world' (Bundy 1947: 1). Many problems could be dealt with through the application of science and expertise.

International organization, as a process within world politics identified by scholars, was understood according to Hewson (2008: 6) to mean that suprastate institutions such as the United Nations would in time become more numerous and tackle more tasks, have more authority in relation to states, and be 'more systematic, rational, and organized'. International organization, unlike the idealism of the interwar years, was prominent as an organizing concept in a period of strong hegemonic leadership by the United States. The concept of international organization, as practically deployed, was not divorced from the reality of great-power politics and leadership. At the time, the United States led the world in productive capacity, scientific research, military potency and technological know-how. The United States alone had the resources to fund balance-of-payments adjustment in Europe, aiding these states to restart world trade. This gave the United States a major advantage in the negotiation of new international regimes, such as that for air travel. But without the leadership of the United States, resources for the establishment of international organization in the 1940s would have been few and far between.

The reality of hegemonic leadership behind international organization meant that, despite the ambition to solve problems, the organizing concept or process of international organization was always limited in that it reflected the core interests of the richest and most powerful states. Not surprisingly, the core states were largely satisfied with the way international relations was organized and major problems were addressed. They were interested in refining and developing systems and institutions, but not in remaking the world order into a fairer, less exploitative place. In this sense, international organization was what Cox, following the Frankfurt School of social theory, has called a 'problem-solving concept' (Cox with Sinclair 1996: 88). International organization was plainly not an idea of how international relations should be re-organized, a critical concept that could form the intellectual basis for a fundamental rethinking of how the world was governed. It could never become the basis for the change sought by Henry and Sofia Mason.

Failure of international organization

The idea of international organization, understood here as an organizing principle, or overarching framework of international relations, fell into disfavour in the 1960s and 1970s. In Africa and Asia, new states emerged from European colonial control in the late 1950s and 1960s. The end of colonialism had a major impact on the institutions of international organization. Discussion took on a decidedly more radical flavour in international fora. New agendas came to the fore in the UN and its specialist agencies, including, importantly, the idea of a New International Economic Order (NIEO) between North and South. The NIEO called for a major redistribution of resources between rich and poor. During this period the non-aligned bloc developed, and UN General Assembly votes increasingly reflected the views of the world's poor rather than those of the hegemonic states of the rich North.

The late 1960s and 1970s were also a time in which American hegemony experienced relative decline. This was hardly a surprise given that the US economy had amounted to nearly half of world GDP in 1945 at the end of the most deadly conflict in history. But relative decline was significant for the direction of US policy. Writers such as Strange (1994) have suggested that this period sees the onset of a more unilateral self-interested policy on the part of the United States. This development generated overt hostility to the US even amongst rich nations. A feature of this tendency was the US policy of printing dollars to finance both the Vietnam War and the Great Society welfare programmes of the second half of the 1960s. This flood of dollars stimulated inflation and this contributed to a decade or more of economic policy problems for industrial countries.

The new assertiveness of the post-colonial societies eager to redress past wrongs came at the same time as the industrial countries experienced these tensions with US leadership. Things that had seemed technical matters after victory in the 1940s were no longer so easy. Conflicts over economic resources, rules for trade and finance, and the operation of the UN and its agencies themselves became endemic. These were fundamentally political conflicts. The United States, or at least parts of the US Government, became increasingly uncomfortable with the views expressed in the UN and championed within multilateral organizations. During the 1980s, the US grew tardy in funding the organization, and debates within Congress sought linkage between US payments and reforms in UN operations.

From the late 1960s, the idea of international organization fell into disuse. *International Organization*, the journal which carried this name founded in the 1940s, increasingly drew back from matters of international policy and instead became a vehicle for the development of rigorous academic theorizing. It seemed that the idea of international organization understood as a policy goal was no longer feasible. The concept belonged to an earlier, more optimistic and more hegemonic age. The realities of the world of the 1970s were not ones in which the concept, as an organizing principle for international relations, could thrive.

New challenges

The abandonment of the idea of international organization signalled the end of faith in the post-war dream of a world in which states could plan their way out of conflict and into peaceful prosperity. International organization had proven to be a notion closely associated with the confidence of victory that could not address new, unanticipated conflicts and challenges to the prevailing world order. But despite the failure of international organization as a concept and a reality, the debate about managing international affairs did not cease. Several new challenges came together in the 1970s and 1980s to rekindle the ambition that had underpinned the idea of a system of international organization.

The Bretton Woods system of fixed exchange rates had come to an end in 1971 because of the imbalance between US gold stocks and increasing external US dollar holdings created to finance war and the 1960s social programmes, without a commensurate increase in the US tax burden. Bretton Woods had been created at the end of 1944 and was a key element in the effort to build international organization. Its purpose was to facilitate the balancing of liabilities between countries without the need for states to deflate their economies, putting people out of work. This sort of contraction in economic activity had been the normal way in which countries adjusted to each other during the era of the gold standard prior to World War I. The architects of Bretton Woods saw this adjustment process as politically impossible after World War II, given the heightened expectations of returning soldiers and their families for a good, secure life. The planners were also keen to avoid the return of destabilizing capital flows between societies, which they blamed for the development of trade friction between the wars.

The end of Bretton Woods, and the re-emergence of global finance in the 1970s and 1980s, characterized by increasingly free capital movement, created significant problems. Volatility, especially in exchange rates, was a great concern in the 1970s and 1980s. Europeans, in particular, were concerned about the negative implications of floating currencies. For them, the attractions of a more ordered world were very strong. This anxiety produced the Basle capital accord of 1986, which regulated the reserves that banks had to hold to support their lending. The 1980s was also a time in which cooperation between rich-country central banks became increasingly formalized.

Another key challenge that emerged in the 1970s and 1980s was the environment (Carter 2010). While anti-pollution measures were not new – England had put in place clean air laws in the 1950s to beat the killer London smogs – an awareness of the transborder nature of environmental problems was novel. This was illustrated by the case of acid rain created by 'dirty' coal-burning power stations in the US. Although created in the US, much of the acid rain actually fell on lakes in Canada, poisoning fish and plant life, killing the ecosystem of many waterways. One key product of this challenge was the United Nations Conference on Environment and Development (UNCED), held in Rio de Janeiro, in June 1992.

The Less Developed Country (LDC) debt crisis of the 1980s was a crucial moment in the development of new ideas about global management. The crisis had its origins in the desire of many developing states to avoid borrowing from the International Monetary Fund (IMF) and World Bank. Official lending came with conditions that sought to limit what the LDCs could do with the money they had borrowed. Private-sector money did not have the same conditionality attached and was very plentiful in the mid-1970s because of the massive rise in the price of oil. These 'petrodollars' were deposited in western banks that needed to find a way to earn income on these funds. As a result, credit standards fell and many loans were made that would not have been made, had there not been such a flood of money. Because inflation was high during this period, the money was borrowed by the LDCs in the form of floating rate loans. When interest rates rose, so would the rates on these loans. The rise in rates, when it came in 1979 toward the end of the Carter presidency, has come to be known as the 'Volker shift' after chairman of the Federal Reserve, Paul Volker. This effort to tackle inflation helped to create a severe recession in the early 1980s and a collapse in international commodity prices. By the early 1980s, the LDCs were paying much more for their loans, but their exports had collapsed in volume and value because of weak demand in the recession-hit rich countries. So costs were up at the same time as income was down. The debt crisis developed rapidly, not just creating severe problems for these countries, but destroying the balance sheets of many rich-country banks, threatening the functioning of the global financial system. Ironically, this effort on the part of LDCs to get around the restrictions of the international financial institutions had the opposite effect and helped alter substantially the receptiveness of these states to market-based solutions to their problems during the 1990s. By exhausting the idea of home-grown strategies, the LDC debt crisis created the right conditions for an even more invasive programme of scrutiny than these countries had experienced previously.

The idea of global governance

These problems, and many others such as human rights, land-mine clearance and migration, made policy-analysts and academics alike think again about the management of global problems. These issues were familiar to John and Helen Mason and Agastya and Bhadraa Patel. International organization had been too ambitious a notion, and too explicitly linked to the prevailing pattern of American hegemony in the context of an ongoing Cold War. What was needed in the new conditions following the end of the Cold War was a more pragmatic idea, one that was not dependent on the support of one key state, and an idea that was focused on outcomes rather than just institutional processes.

The first widely circulated statement that used the concept of global governance is found in the report of the Commission on Global Governance, published as *Our Global*

Neighborhood (Commission on Global Governance 1995).
Stimulated by the end of the Cold War and what the Commission termed a 'heightened sense' of an 'endangered future' (Commission 1995: xix), the report asserted that governance 'is the sum of the many ways individuals and institutions, public and private, manage their common affairs' (Commission 1995: 2). The Commission's report appears to be a management vision of global governance, one concerned with dealing with feasible, tractable problems, rather than broad issues of blame for poverty and exploitation, or adjustment of the prevailing world order. Explicitly political dimensions of the relations between rich and poor states seem to be minimized by deploying this implicitly managerial concept.

A central feature of global governance as articulated by the Commission was the role of private, non-state institutions in the creation and enforcement of governance. Economic integration, especially the growth of capital markets, had created a multitude of new actors. In some cases, the Commission suggested, governance would rely on markets and market institutions, 'perhaps with some institutional oversight' (Commission 1995: 5). The incorporation of private sources of governance, such as NGOs, citizens' movements and Multinational Corporations (MNCs), was necessary now in order to acknowledge the broader scope of governance after the Cold War. Previously, governance at the international level had primarily been understood as a consequence of intergovernmental relations. Accepting the role of private institutions in governance would, suggested the Commission, increase their effectiveness. But emphasis on these newly relevant private sources of governance fitted neatly into a more managerial vision of how to deal with global problems. The management focus of the global governance concept, as articulated by these international policy-makers, was reinforced by the priority given to private agents, because private agents are not – in the common-sense understanding of the term – political. They are, by their nature, technical. Even if they are lobby groups like NGOs, the main focus of these private institutions is on practical projects, not political change.

During the 1990s, the concept of global governance became part of the lexicon of the development policy community, including the international financial institutions, NGOs, think tanks, government agencies and academics (Payne and Phillips 2010). It has become the term of choice because it captures what Hewson has identified as the 'essential property of global governance: the creation of at least some degree of *political union* in place of political division on a worldwide scale' (Hewson 2008: 1), and at the same time avoids the unequivocally political connotations of 'government', and the even worse implications of other labels, such as 'power' and 'authority'. It seemingly provides a non-emotive concept around which major issues of societal rule can be deliberated by experts and officials, without making explicit what is implicit in the idea of global governance, namely the political conflict and struggle which underpin any system of rule. Global governance seems safe, balanced and neutral. As formulated like this, global governance had major appeal to the Patel and Mason families.

Key institutions of global governance

Most people are likely to think of international institutions, or 'global governors', when the question of global governance is raised (Avant, Finnemore and Sell 2010). In addition to these traditional intergovernmental organizations, Scholte identifies five further institutional mechanisms: transgovernmental, inter-regional, translocal, private and public–private hybrids (Scholte 2011: 11). The major intergovernmental organizations include the Organization of American States, the Universal Postal Union, and the United Nations and its constituent agencies. There were 238 intergovernmental organizations at the start of the new millennium (Karns and Mingst 2009: 7). Intergovernmental organizations serve different purposes including: gathering information (UN Environmental Programme); providing services (UN High Commissioner for Refugees); creating a space for intrastate bargaining (European Union); settling disputes (International Court of Justice) amongst others (Karns and Mingst 2009: 7). The power of intergovernmental organizations is largely informal and rests on the mutual benefits from conformity to the system (Karns and Mingst 2009: 9).

A very high profile sub-set of key intergovernmental organizations consists of the multilateral economic institutions (O'Brien et al. 2000: 2; Chwieroth 2009; Higgott 2010). These, in particular the IMF, the World Bank and World Trade Organization (WTO, founded in 1995), are the subject of heated debate about their policies and operating procedures, especially amongst developing countries and their advocates (Wilkinson 2006; Koppell 2010). The IMF was established to smooth international adjustment in the balance of payments between countries. When a deficit occurred in a country's national accounts, and exports failed to pay for a country's imports, the idea was that, rather than devalue its currency, a country could call on the IMF to help it, avoiding any dramatic domestic political conflict and potential beggarthy-neighbour devaluations by other states. From the 1980s onwards, IMF policy shifted toward a more market-friendly position encouraging, rather than shielding states from, adjustment, especially the newly emerging economies. The World Bank had been founded initially to help Europe reconstruct after the devastation of World War II. After this job was done it turned to assisting developing countries to foster economic growth, increasingly putting conditions on loans that mandated market-friendly reforms. It seems clear that the existence and work of these institutions is a major reason there is so much interest in the concept of global governance. The Patels in particular, like many families in the developing world, are keenly aware of the work of the multilateral economic organizations.

The other thing that comes to mind most readily when thinking of key institutions of global governance is international law, especially treaty law between states (Simmons and Steinberg 2006). Examples include arms control agreements, intellectual property law, law of the sea, and whaling and other environmental treaties (Karns and Mingst 2009: 5). In addition to readily identifiable interstate agreements, there is also extensive 'soft law' in the form of norms and standards of behaviour in many substantive areas such as human rights and labour rights (Risse, Ropp and Sikkink 1999; Karns and Mingst 2009: 6). The big issue with international law, which challenges the very idea that it is law, is the question of enforcement. Inside states, law binds citizens who have no choice but to obey or be subject to punishment. Because there is no world government over and above individual states, governments must in effect agree to be bound by international law. Whether international law is 'law' at all in the absence of binding constraints is an open question. For people like John Mason, and millions of others like him, raised to respect the law and due process, a legal basis to global rule seems enormously appealing.

Increasingly prominent are private voluntary organizations, active usually in specific issue areas. These organizations, also known as global social movements, include the World Wildlife Fund, Oxfam, Transparency International and Amnesty International (O'Brien et al. 2000: 2). What is distinctive about them is that they add a non-governmental voice to debates about major problems that would otherwise be dominated by the richest and most powerful states. However, as global social movements are self-appointed, substantial questions about their democratic legitimacy inevitably arise (Scholte 2011).

Often excluded from discussions of global governance, major international business corporations may also be considered key institutions of global governance in three ways. First, multinational corporations are highly consequential for everyday life in developed and developing countries; second, they are continuously involved in lobbying government for better regulation and government oversight of markets domestically and internationally; and last, because regulation, or self-regulation, is often undertaken by market agents themselves, business is increasingly governing many fields. Like other institutions or actors within global governance, we will find that different perspectives put greater or lesser emphasis on business corporations.

Within the broader set of private authorities, following Murphy (2000) and Sinclair (2005), we can identify those that 'regulate both states and much of transnational economic and social life' (Murphy 2000: 793). Credit rating agencies are an example mentioned by Murphy, whose work shapes government policies. These agencies examine the creditworthiness of borrowing states and corporations. The agencies investigate ability to pay, and, in the case of countries, the willingness to pay, given that sovereign borrowers are in a good position to repudiate debts if they should so wish. What intrigues analysts are the subjectivity of the judgements involved and the great consequences of the work of the agencies in terms of raising the price of borrowing and potentially in cutting off access to it altogether. In addition to credit rating agencies can be added the societies which regulate the work of physicians, lawyers and other professionals, consumer protection agencies which rate and judge products and services, and other intermediaries that operate in modern markets to do obscure things like regulate domain name distribution in the internet or the quality of plumbing work, and create rating and ranking systems for university programmes. Most of these forms of private quasi-regulation involve the application of judgement, the accountability of which is unclear.

Key issues for global governance

Perhaps for most people what makes them interested in global governance is the potential it offers to deal with problems and issues that they think are important. The Patels and Masons share this predisposition. One of the most acute issues in global governance in recent years is the global financial crisis that began in the summer of 2007 (Gamble 2009; Germain 2010). The crisis, which began after several years of booming housing and financial markets, has demonstrated how important global financial stability is for sustained prosperity. Initial hopes that developing countries would somehow be shielded from the fallout proved unfounded, giving rise to recessionary conditions almost everywhere. The crisis raises issues of coordination of the immediate response to the unprecedented loss of confidence in securities markets, and longer-term reconsideration of the regulatory governance framework for finance.

A central issue in global governance are the inequalities in wealth and growth that divide the rich nations of the North or developed world from the relatively poorer states of the developing South. These disparities are huge. Murphy notes that almost half the human population lives on less than $2 a day (Murphy 2000: 791). Held observes that 'the absolute gap between the world's richest and poorest states is now the largest it has been' (Held 2004: 35). These hardships are experienced most acutely by women, who comprise 70 per cent of the 1.2 billion living on less than $1 a day (Held 2004: 37).

Security is, of course, a perennial concern in international politics, and very much at the heart of most schemas of global governance. Cold War concerns about nuclear war were followed, after the East–West confrontation had ended, by the idea, popular for a while, that no viable alternative existed to Liberal capitalism (Fukuyama 1992). This 'end of history thesis' was forgotten with the atrocities of 11 September 2001 and the onset of global concerns about terrorism inspired by radical Islam. The subsequent invasions of Afghanistan in 2001, and especially Iraq in 2003, raised grave concerns about unilateral US action. It is likely that these experiences will lead to more efforts at multilateral approaches to security threats of this kind.

Global warming is something few can be unaware of today. Domestically, governments are well placed to legislate and enforce environmental standards through law and institutional change (Ostrom 1990; Ellickson 1991). The reason that environmental issues are matters for global governance is that countries are not closed environmental systems. Emissions in one territory may well affect conditions elsewhere and for the planet as a whole. In a sense, these emissions are part of the cost (or consequences) of human activity on the planet, but large creators of emissions may not face these costs directly themselves. A major part of the impetus behind the global governance debate is to close this 'loop hole' and force those who create these externalities to face up to the costs they have created for others (Drezner 2007).

Gender and the rights of women are major issues in some accounts of global governance (Rai and Waylen 2008a). Like most systems of power, global governance has been dominated by men. This can mean that senior offices are dominated by men or that the logic of institutions and procedures are developed with masculine assumptions. One of the things that separates different approaches to global governance is how the gender issue is regarded and the different values placed on female emancipation.

One of the complexities of global governance is that it involves many different kinds of actors working together. Although states and their relations are very much at the heart of international relations, the nature of many issues means that non-state actors and corporations work with international organizations and specific states. This inevitably creates coordination problems that do not exist in relations between states alone. Although global governance may hold out the promise of more effective and deeper solutions to problems, it also contains inherent risks of conflict and failure that arise from its constitutional complexity.

Environmental anxieties like those just discussed, financial crises, industrial restructuring and cross-border migration have combined to create increasing uncertainty in both developed and developing societies (Beck 1992; Sassen 1998). At many levels the certainties of the mass production and mass consumption societies that dominated the years after World War II have come unstuck in the developed world. This new world, in which sovereign states do not have all the answers, and in which interdependency seems to be increasing, poses considerable problems for the domestic systems of government that have evolved since the age of Enlightenment in the eighteenth century. In this context, it is hardly surprising that there has been much interest in creating new, better-adapted systems of rule.

Despite the perception that our systems of rule are out of date given the problems that confront us, a major issue for architects of global governance is the question of who exercises governance, and for whom global governance is done. The question here is whether global governance is going to be controlled by experts, who will typically be in rich countries, or whether developing nations should exercise control themselves, in their interest. This is not a new debate, and it increasingly came to dominate international organizations from the late 1960s onwards. It led to an entire tradition in international relations and international political economy which premised its analytical insight on the perception of fundamental disparities between core, metropolitan states and those marginalized, on the periphery (Chang and Grabel

2004). The struggle over control and over the purposes of global governance remains as central now as it was to international relations two generations ago.

Power, authority and global governance

Power is never far away in any discussion of global governance. A simple way to understand power is as the ability to get someone to do what they otherwise would not do (Lukes 1986: 2). This is certainly a useful way to identify power. Power can also be seen written into the way things are organized in the world. The fact that a smaller or poorer country must operate within systems and procedures written by larger and richer states can be thought of in power terms. In this case, the power, or structural power as Strange termed it, 'confers the power to decide how things shall be done, the power to shape frameworks within which states relate to each other, relate to people, or relate to corporate enterprises' (Strange 1994: 25). Barnett and Duvall's (2005: 46) 'productive power' is a more diffuse view of structural power, which acknowledges the effect of power in actually shaping the identities of the parties involved, disciplining them, making them into what they become.

If power is not always explicit or obvious, this is even more the case with authority. For many people, authority refers simply to the law. A police officer has the authority of the law and may use coercion to enforce it. But as we have seen, in the world of global governance, clear legal authority for action is often lacking. Authority in another sense, however, is very applicable. This sense of authority refers to the wisdom or experience of the individual or institution, and lacks any coercive or enforcement dimension. This sense of authority relates to the accuracy or reliability of the judgements of those with authority (Friedman 1990: 63–4), and the esteem in which they are held.

Given the emphasis on the private realm and the lack of overarching legal authority, it seems that global governance is much more dependent on epistemic authority than international organization, which drew expertise into the major international institutions. At first glance this seems to make global governance much more vulnerable than international organization because of the dependence of global governance on something as ephemeral as reputation and wisdom. But if you look at this another way, the base for the legitimacy of global governance is much wider and less vulnerable to criticisms compared with international organization, premised on US hegemony. Even if specific institutions lose their epistemic authority and can no longer serve to maintain global governance, the problem can be defined as a technical one rather than one of fundamental political order (Burnham 1999).

Governance, like authority of the epistemic variety, has to be distinguished from its obvious formal legal twin, government (Rosenau 1992). Government, which imposes a system of rule over a state, has sovereignty in that there is no formal level of authority (in the legal sense) able to override its decisions in its own domestic sphere. Governance is concerned with effective rule. Governments have formal authority, but some cannot exercise this very effectively and have little ability to impose their laws on their own citizens. As governments, they have weak powers of governance.

Lacking world government, this inability to rule in the formal sense means that there is no government over global relations. But governance, when used as part of the term 'global governance', suggests that the informal, sub- or supra-governmental systems it comprises may actually be better adapted for a world of new challenges than the formal legal mechanisms of government. So, global governance should not be understood as a weaker or less developed system of rule because it lacks a unified government. Although global governance may seem amorphous, it operates at more levels than formal systems (Kjaer 2004). Although raised to recognize and respect legal authority, both the Patel and Mason families, like people everywhere, are slowly waking up to the idea that global power is increasingly exercised in new ways. This excites them as they contemplate a world of change and new possibilities, on the one hand, and somewhat unnerves them too, as they come to realize that the world of certainties they were raised in seems to be gone. What influence they and people like them will have in this new world is unclear.

We need to acknowledge the potential for less desirable forms of global governance to develop. I have already mentioned the example of private credit rating agencies as a form of quasi-regulation. While rating agencies may serve a useful purpose in providing information to investors, they do have the potential to be procyclical – that is, to make a crisis worse than it already is by highlighting latent problems, as seems to have been the case in the Euro zone sovereign debt crisis that began in 2009. So, while the individual merits of rating information to each investor can be useful, the collective effect can be to worsen circumstances and make the crisis much worse than it would have otherwise been. Given the potential for the development of quasi-regulation in global governance to depoliticize, and thus remove controversial issues from public debate, the growth of this form of global governance might be attractive to some but potentially negative for many.

Overall comments

This chapter considered the basis of the post-war global order and how the idea of international organization as a unifying process was thought key to addressing the problems of the period after World War II. International organization was an ambitious notion, premised on US hegemony. The chapter then examined how the notion of international organization broke down under the new strains created by the ending of colonial empires and the relative decline of the US. International organization offered too much and delivered too little. But coping with new challenges – while acknowledging the problems of international organization – led to the further development of notions of international cooperation into the idea of global governance. The origins of global governance lie in the search for a more feasible, less ambitious order focused on management, the acceptance of scarcity and the avoidance of dependence on US power. A major feature of global governance is its emphasis on private mechanisms, given the political controversy that has enveloped especially the major international economic and financial institutions such as the IMF and World Bank. The chapter then discussed some of the core institutions of global governance typically found in most accounts, some of the key issues that animate debate about global governance, and some of the core concepts that are essential to an appreciation of global governance and its limits. In the next chapter we will consider the first perspective on global governance, as it permeates official circles.

3
Institutionalism

In everyday conversation, global governance is most often equated with institutions such as the United Nations, the IMF and the World Bank. These institutions are well known and are what people think of when they talk about international institutions. These are the institutions of the post-World War II system of international organization considered in chapter 2.

Given that the term 'global governance' has its origins in the work of these international or supranational institutions, perhaps this usage is not surprising. It is hardly a surprise either that institutions, including these, feature in all conceptions of global governance to a greater or lesser extent, as you will see in subsequent chapters of this book. Institutionalism, as a perspective on global governance, is concerned with institutions and the people who staff them as the central feature of global governance. Institutionalism focuses on the organizations, the office holders and the interactions between institutions deemed central to global governance. This approach and field of study is sometimes referred to as the study of international organization or international institutions, typically linked to Liberal approaches to international relations. In this focus it shares something with all the other ways of thinking considered in this book, but in its very limited purpose it is at odds with Transnationalism, Cosmopolitanism, Hegemonism, Feminism and Rejectionism.

For some Institutionalists, technocrats or experts have a central role in the running of a complex world as elected and appointed officials (Cox and Jacobson 1973). Their work as politicians and bureaucrats helps to manage the regimes that facilitate trade, finance poverty reduction and allow long-distance telephone calls to connect across the globe. Much of this work involves thinking through how new challenges such as nuclear weapons proliferation or water shortages might be dealt with through international cooperation and the provision of resources. Their understanding of global governance is central to the advice they offer.

Policy-making and its implementation via intergovernmental institutions are central to the development of global governance as understood by Institutionalism. This chapter explores how technocrats working in important institutions such as the Universal Postal Union and the World Bank understand global governance, and the significance of the concept for their work. Importantly, as is the case in the following chapters, the attention here is necessarily on the main tendency and not on all the possible variations that might exist.

What is appealing about this perspective? The short answer is that it seems intuitive and relatively simple. It equates power and control with mostly well-known institutions and the people who run them. For the analyst, the citizen and the student, making the assumption that a small set of institutions run the world is easily done, and pointing to the institutions themselves is similarly simple to do. This seemingly straightforward way of thinking about global governance gives this perspective on the concept a large audience and makes it by far the most popular and widespread view considered in this book. But institutions are not as straightforward as is often assumed. Indeed, they are very complex and counter-intuitive. The very appeal of this approach can potentially pose problems because it does not require a shift in thinking and so tends not to challenge everyday prejudice about global politics and how institutions work.

Background

As we saw in chapter 2, the victorious Allied nations established a whole new architecture of interstate coordination at the end of World War II, called the United Nations system, inheriting some organizations such as the International Labour Office from the defunct League of Nations and creating many others. This plethora of international institutions has operated for approaching seventy years and has become a significant part of how our world is run. But this system was designed for a world in which production and consumption were more nationally isolated and independent than they are in the world we live in. The everyday assumptions about a world of international institutions at the centre of global governance have been challenged by change. The world of the twenty-first century is not the same as that of 1944, and this puts institutions designed for that earlier world under some pressure. Globalization has altered the context in which technocrats conceive institutions of global governance (Mittelman 2000; Held and Koenig-Archibugi 2003; Scholte 2005). Although this is at times exaggerated, the world has become more interconnected since the end of the Bretton Woods regime in the early 1970s. The era of international organization was a time of Cold War, high tariff barriers, protectionism, balance-of-payments crises and relatively limited information flows. Despite the recent global financial crisis that started in 2007, increasingly, money flows across borders free of state control, goods are easily traded and technology exchanged with few barriers in the developed world. This interconnectedness and the cross-border nature of major new problems like climate change challenges the position of national governments and enhances the power of private agents (Held et al. 1999: 10). This change undermines inherited assumptions about what actually comprise the core features of global governance.

One of the major features of this movement toward a globalized planet has been the rise of doctrines that advocate a more liberalized world, in which markets and market institutions have greater freedom of action and more influence over the lives of communities. These views were very popular during the gold-standard era that preceded the First World War and became popular again as the mixed economy created after the Second World War ran into inflation and low productivity growth starting in the late 1960s. Prime Minister Margaret Thatcher in Britain and President Ronald Reagan in the United States popularized these ideas in the 1980s. In this neo-liberal view, markets and market institutions are usually thought to be more efficient at providing services and solving problems than public bureaucracies. In a number of ways the neo-liberal worldview encapsulates and popularizes some doctrines of orthodox economics (Rhoads 1985). In the world of the technocratic policy elites, these ideas have been termed the 'Washington Consensus' (Williamson 1994: 26–8). Central ideas in the Washington Consensus are control over public spending, the usefulness of tax cuts, liberalization of financial markets, trade liberalization, deregulation, privatization and legally enforceable property rights. Faced with opposition, especially from developing nations, these ideas have been modified somewhat with new emphasis on good governance, understood as accountability and fairness in intergovernmental organizations (Woods 1999: 41; Soederberg 2006: 36). Despite these modifications, the core emphasis on the value of markets remains (Griffin 2006: 573) and is likely to outlive financial turbulence given the lack of well-conceived alternatives.

Purpose

'Global governance' is not merely a descriptive label used by policy-makers, like 'international institutions'. In the contemporary context of change and reform, Institutionalism conceives of global governance in purposeful terms. For them, global governance is part of a practical way of thinking about the problems they are trying to solve. Global governance is not, for these officials, about transforming the facts of life of the world order we know. It is about making that existing order work better than it does now. In this sense, Institutionalism's approach to global governance has a problem-solving rather than critical purpose (Cox with Sinclair 1996: 88). Problem-solving does not preclude politics. Officials who use the term 'global governance' are using it in Dingwerth and Pattberg's sense of a political programme to further reform and make the world better (2006: 193). But technocrats fundamentally take the structure of the world as given and not subject to transformation. The limited purpose of this conception of global governance can be illustrated by example. Since the 1950s, developing countries – most of which were colonized by the western powers in the nineteenth and early twentieth centuries – have complained about unfair terms of trade for their goods and the disadvantage they face in dealing with interstate institutions dominated by the rich countries. A critical conception of this problem suggests the need to eliminate the causes of inequality and thus unfairness in the world. This might mean a wholesale remake of global institutions and perhaps a challenge to capitalism as we know it. Institutionalism takes a very different approach. Distrustful of such big and disruptive solutions, it looks for smaller, less threatening change that might put developing countries on the road to prosperity. The status quo – such as capitalism and private property – is preserved, but the chances of achieving success in this framework are enhanced.

Given the problem-solving agenda of Institutionalism, it seems fair to characterize the approach as conservative in the sense that change is pursued within the fundamental norms we know, in such a way as to avoid upsetting the major stakeholders of the system (such as property owners). We should not, however, see the approach as merely incremental because of this. Small changes, such as introducing more market-based norms like paying for things that were previously provided free by the state, can cause enormous dislocation to the wider population, as when municipal water charges, for example, have been introduced in developing countries.

Puzzles

The key issue for Institutionalism is how to make global governance function better in pursuit of technocratic goals, from delivering an international telephone service and air travel safety, to the development of clean drinking-water supplies in South Asia. Taking the broad outlines of the world system as given and immutable in a practical sense, the puzzle that follows for the technocrats is the exact nature and arrangement of institutions and processes required to generate the outcome required (Koremenos, Lipson and Snidal 2004; Hawkins et al. 2006). At one level then, global governance, for technocrats at least, is a fairly mundane – although challenging – question of the machinery of government, but considered in this case in the broader sphere of global relations, where the enforcement of laws by sovereign governments is not possible. Instead, governance by a range of institutions, public and now increasingly private, domestic and international, is characteristic.

Key subsidiary questions for Institutionalism include the implications of globalization for the work of international institutions, especially dealing with the uncertainties created by the increasing prominence of new actors like NGOs and private expert agencies. Given that the major intergovernmental organizations have their origins in the post-World War II era, it is no wonder the global governance issues are now so acute. In the 1950s and 1960s, officials did not have to deal with competing and sometimes better-resourced private agencies.

Dealing with the externalities of globalization, such as transborder pollution and climate change, outsourcing and migration, fully engages Institutionalism. The questions for officials revolve around how to coordinate action by intergovernmental organizations, states and non-state organizations to understand and find solutions to these problems that affect us all.

A further major problem for the technocrats is how to legitimate or sell global governance. As we will see in chapter 8, global governance is not a universal objective, and many have a sceptical view of the idea, from a variety of different political positions. Much of this reflects deeply held commitments to national determination and sovereignty, reinforced in the years following World War II. Technocrats who take global externalities like pollution and their control seriously must also take the political support – or lack of it – for global governance seriously too.

Level of analysis and actors

For Institutionalism, global governance provides the means through which, at the broadest level, what technocrats do is organized, resourced and legitimated to the wider public. Global governance functions as a level of international cooperation between governments over tractable problems in the absence of a central world government over and above sovereign states. Although global governance is more than simply another name for international institutions in Institutionalism, it is at the level of intergovernmental cooperation that the major action occurs for Institutionalism, so this is where global governance takes place in this conception. Global governance is largely a VIP-suite phenomenon here, a matter of expert advice and executive political decisions.

Given this focus on expert advice and executive political decisions, the key actors concerned with global governance for Institutionalism are the personnel of large government and intergovernmental organizations. When pushed, Institutionalism will accept a role for the more successful NGOs too.

The important point is that a clear distinction is drawn in Institutionalism between those who make global governance – high elected and appointed officials – and those who receive, or are subject to, global governance (the rest of us). In Institutionalism, the citizenry in both developed and developing countries is clearly subject to global governance and understood as having little opportunity to shape decisions or understand the issues involved.

In the real world, this might mean that analysts and policy-advisers who think in these terms have an inherent tendency to discount or neglect the broader context of global relations, given their concern with the action concentrated in elite networks. This could put a premium on policy advice that 'works' in the sense that it is enacted by decision-makers in institutions. Whether this advice works in the broader sense is another matter. Political scientists like Graham Allison have studied the dynamics of bureaucratic politics and decision-making in institutions for many years, and have found that, even in dire situations like war, these internal concerns often dominate the work of institutions (Allison and Zelikow 1999). It is as if in these modern institutions there is still a concern with what is going on at 'Court' and a disregard for what is actually happening in the world. Given this internal focus of actors on the level of elite interaction, it is easy to imagine that the global focus on what is happening in the world can get lost.

Assumptions

Given the above understanding of the key actors, a primary assumption of Institutionalism about global governance is that it is an executive process, far removed from any real possibility of mass participation. Global governance is patently not a popular phenomenon in this view.

Institutionalism assumes international organizations can have a relatively autonomous influence on the world. They are not merely the creatures of states, but have their own authority (Barnett and Finnemore 2004: 5). From this, it follows that their internal bureaucratic processes matter (Barnett and Finnemore 2004: 3).

Institutionalism assumes that global governance is a limited idea, suited to solving problems within a prevailing world order. Global governance is about managing problems, rather than eliminating fundamental causes of problems.

Another key assumption made in Institutionalism is that global governance is, or should be, driven by expertise, knowledge and science (Stone 1996). The academic discipline of economics has a privileged place in contemporary policy debates. While it is not possible to solve the world's problems in any structural or enduring sense for Institutionalism, science and learning are the basis for problem-solving in the real world.

For technocrats, the neo-liberal set of ideas is not an ideology, but a programme of well-developed reform initiatives based on many years of experience dealing with the deep-seated problems in developed and less developed countries. Technocrats do not identify neo-liberalism as a political programme (Griffin 2006: 575). Instead, growth, conceived in simple quantitative terms, is understood to be the primary route to solving problems through development.

Politics, in the sense of democratic choice, must be acknowledged as it is a force to be dealt with in governing the world. But given the technocratic commitment to expertise in Institutionalism, politics is often seen as an obstruction, especially when dealing with developing states.

Ontology

Several things are of significance in this conception of global governance. Governments are clearly privileged in this understanding. That is not to say that other stakeholders are irrelevant. It is just that, in the technocratic vision of Institutionalism, government and intergovernmental agencies come first. So, despite acknowledgement of new forms of governance, states remain central to this conception of global governance (Slaughter 2004; Stone 2011).

This conception of global governance places primary emphasis on knowledge as a source of influence and persuasion. Although governance here is backed by government, what gives global governance its salience is not coercion and compulsion, but superior knowledge and insight. In other words, this notion of global governance places a premium on authority understood as stemming from experience and knowledge.

Although this is a non-coercive conception, its authority, like that of a judge, is backed by law. As I discussed in chapter 2, law is useful as a way of promoting and enacting global governance. New regulation, in particular, is thought to spread better approaches to policy in a given issue area such as transport or health.

Education and the development of human capital are key things to focus upon in the refinement and improvement of the human condition in Institutionalism. This stems from the assumption that the world can be improved, albeit gradually, within limits.

Implications

A key consequence of the assumptions behind this conception of global governance is that global governance is really a matter to be reserved for very well-educated experts, and that ordinary people cannot and should not make a substantial contribution. Global governance is understood to be an elite, expert phenomenon.

Given the focus on a limited problem-solving agenda, there is an unwillingness to consider deeper, more structural issues of inequality that may shape outcomes for developing countries. This conception of global governance could be thought of as limited or restricted, and as reproducing the broad parameters or status quo of the world order as constituted.

Given the championing of a neo-liberal agenda, despite the modifications to this worldview with the incorporation of good governance, other policy choices and the social and political agendas they represent are necessarily downplayed or disadvantaged. Because of this, one implication of Institutionalism's conception of global governance is an inherent political conservatism.

Applications

The most celebrated or notorious concrete manifestation of Institutionalism's conception of global governance must be in the policy scrutiny applied by the international financial institutions, the IMF and the World Bank. Throughout the 1980s and 1990s, the international financial institutions pursued a policy agenda guided by Washington Consensus prescriptions, based on very strong assumptions about the merits of elite expertise.

Two applications stand out during these decades. The first is the Latin American debt crisis of the 1980s. The other is the response to the Asian financial crisis of 1997/8. The Latin American debt crisis of the 1980s occurred because developing countries in Latin America borrowed heavily from banks during the 1970s for investment in their own economic growth. With the 1973 oil crisis and the quadrupling of oil prices, western banks were flooded with dollar deposits. Banks were eager to lend these deposits out and were less scrupulous about creditworthiness than usual. The strategy of borrowing from private-sector banks was motivated by a desire on the part of developing countries to avoid the constraints of official borrowing from the IMF and World Bank. Unfortunately, timing was not on the side of these countries. Inflation, floating interest rates, recession and falls in commodity prices conspired to increase their debt repayments and reduce their incomes at the same time. The result was defaults on repayment starting in 1982.

These circumstances made developing countries more beholden to the international financial institutions than ever before and greatly increased the importance of these institutions during the 1980s and 1990s. This gave their views about government intervention, which favoured free trade, anti-inflationary monetary policy, low budget deficits and internal market-friendly reform, much greater power than would otherwise have been the case, expanding their significance as agents of global governance. These policy prescriptions, leading as they did to great economic dislocation and change, met with considerable resistance and might be argued to have radicalized politics in many recipient countries, especially in Latin America.

The Asian financial crisis of 1997/8, and how the international financial institutions reacted to it, may turn out to be a significant historical moment. The IMF offered the standard policy formula of floating exchange rates, budget cutting and regulatory reform, even though the problems that precipitated the crisis were to do with short-term borrowing by some financial institutions. Public expenditure was not a big issue in the region and it was not clear how structural reform of this sort was related to the financial crisis. Indeed, the crisis had many of the hallmarks of a classic mania followed by a crash, suggesting much of the blame should have been shared by financial market traders in London and New York. However, as in the Latin American debt crisis, states were forced to follow the IMF line in order to obtain necessary financing during the crisis.

As was the case in Latin America, the approach taken by the IMF, and the necessity to follow this approach, were a cause of much bitterness. As prosperity returned, Asian states began to build their financial reserves and try out new forms of regional cooperation in an effort to avoid being subject to this form of global governance in future. One interpretation of this application of expertise is that, because it took a 'cookie cutter' approach, applying a standard prescription regardless of the specific symptoms, it did not generate the sort of local support it needed to be successful. This suggests expertise does not provide a sufficient basis for global governance, and may indeed be quite destructive of global governance in that, in isolation, it creates opposition and hostility. This highlights the inescapable political character of global governance in a world of sovereign states, in which national populations are bound to resent the coercive application of expertise without their consent.

Differences of emphasis within Institutionalism

The main or dominant tendency in scholarly work on Institutionalism over the last quarter-century has been associated with Robert Keohane. For Keohane and his followers, the focus has been on how the proliferation of organizations and regimes has encouraged the norm of cooperation between states, creating lasting expectations of interdependence (Keohane 1984). Oran Young has extended this work by focusing on the role of non-state actors themselves in extending the scope and effectiveness of regimes (Young 1997). Thomas Weiss has written on overcoming obstacles to effective UN action in addressing major global challenges (Weiss 2012). For him, global governance works well when the UN system works alongside more narrowly based organizations that take care of specialized concerns. Recent work inspired by constructivism in international relations theory has sought to understand international organizations as bureaucracies that develop their own ideas and pursue their own agendas (Barnett and Finnemore 2004).

Strengths

How potent is Institutionalism as a way of thinking about global governance? The intuitive appeal of this way of thinking about global governance is a great strength. Although Institutionalism is a complex and sophisticated worldview, like Realism in international relations theory, it nevertheless appeals to common-sense views of politics in focusing on the role of institutions and elite leaders. This appeal makes Institutionalism the default position on global governance, massively advantaging the conception against others.

As a worldview, this idea of global governance is given strength by its close association with knowledge. In the modern world, knowledge and its acquisition are generally held in high esteem, and the close link between expertise, science and global governance is clearly an analytical and authoritative strength.

A third strength is the limited nature of the concept. This is a problem-solving notion. There is no suggestion here that the world can be restructured from the ground up. Although that makes it very circumscribed, it is precisely this limitation that brings it strength. Global governance, in this conception, seems limited to the sort of change that governments, inter-governmental actors and closely related stakeholders can deliver.

Institutionalism seems to be focused on immediate action. This focus on the present, as opposed to long narratives of past oppression or future hopes, gives the approach a modern and vibrant quality which appeals to those educated in western secular norms. The ability of this way of thinking to 'cut through' to what is essential, casting aside traditional concerns and inclinations, makes it attractive to many in the developing world.

The depoliticized character of Institutionalism's conception of global governance is also a great strength. While Institutionalism does, as we have seen, focus on big, powerful institutions, and elite individuals, it presents its agenda as a technical one, focused on applying science and technological know-how to problems. In this way Institutionalism defuses the accusation that it is a status quo or inequality reinforcing way of thinking about the world.

Weaknesses

What are the vulnerabilities? A major problem with this conception of global governance is that it underestimates the importance of politics in its focus on elite policy preferences. Evidence for this weakness can be observed in the efforts to reformulate the Washington Consensus into a more palatable formulation at the end of the 1990s.

An obvious problem with this view of global governance is that it exaggerates the level of control over policy outcomes likely to be possessed by policy-makers. By neglecting other variables and focusing only on certain elite institutions, it greatly overstates the level of control these institutions possess.

By focusing on the immediate, this approach to global governance ignores deeper and longer-run causes for more proximate problems. Rather than comprehend global governance using a mechanical metaphor, one from the organic world might be more appropriate. This would acknowledge that many problems evolve and their resolution requires a longer-term approach.

By being so neglectful of basic inequalities, such as those surrounding property rights, this way of thinking about global governance neglects the really pressing issues that occupy the attention of billions of people in the developing world. Land tenure is an obvious one, but the problem-solving stance of Institutionalism shies away from such basic issues toward more easily addressed problems.

While the association of Institutionalism with knowledge is certainly a major strength, its neglect of culture and traditional values is problematic. These differences between people are persistent and resistant to change. The unwillingness of the proponents of this approach to global governance to draw this sort of knowledge into their system limits the reception for this conception of global governance.

The intuitive appeal of Institutionalism is also, paradoxically, a weakness, if those who are attracted by this quality do not allow for some of the less intuitive dynamics that permeate all institutions, like competition between them. It may also be the case that the limited conception of global governance proves unable to cope with the externalities generated by climate change and globalization. This conception of global governance takes the system of states we know for granted. But what if this pattern of organization is not adequate for dealing with planet-encompassing issues?

Likely future development

Institutionalism is likely to stress further the importance of expertise, science and technology. After all, these elements are the things that can strengthen elite control over the levers of global power and they are closely linked to control of budget purse strings. They are likely to work best in the context of prosperity and increasing confidence in know-how. This could lead to an increasingly selective and exclusive debate about global governance in which many viewpoints coming from traditional and non-western origins would be deemed illegitimate. Quantitative approaches to knowledge, offering scientistic certainty, will be endorsed over reasoning.

In a second scenario, the rise of non-state or non-governmental expertise increasingly eliminates the claims to expertise and competence made by state and suprastate agents, such as national governments and international institutions. Think of health and food scares and how often governments are powerless to do anything about them. The internet is another sphere in which NGOs may have superior knowledge. Banking and finance are perhaps the supreme example. This scenario would give rise to a genuine change in the basis of global governance. Given what we know of Institutionalism, this is likely to face resistance from states and international institutions.

In the event of further financial crisis or other events not anticipated by expertise, it might be possible to imagine the collapse of the wider public legitimacy of Institutionalism, which, despite it being inattentive to knowledge, is nevertheless necessary for the survival of this worldview. The sort of collapse envisaged would probably be part of a wider crisis of public institutions like those that occurred in the 1930s or in the Arab spring in 2011. These are very rare events reflecting frustration pent up over long periods of time, that then explodes in the context of dramatic policy failure such as the Great Depression, or perhaps the financial crisis that started in 2007.

In the final scenario, the technocrats might try to buy off those parties complaining about their power, putting increasing emphasis on the knowledge dimension of their work, and drawing global civil society into their workings. This is another outcome of crisis. Inviting participation and consultation, offering grants and otherwise buying off dissent are attractive strategies. This is what Cox, drawing on the work of Antonio Gramsci, called 'trasformismo', or 'co-optation'.

Overall comments

Institutionalism is a highly exclusive notion of what global governance is and should be. It assumes that the way to deal with problems that cross borders and that involve multiple nation-states is through the application of expertise by a select few. Although inevitably dependent on politics, this way of thinking neglects politics as a positive force, seeing it as something merely to evade. Inevitably, this suggests either that the benefits of this approach to global governance are few for the many, or that those who take this position do not feel confident about their ability to persuade others of the merits of this approach.

This way of thinking about global governance, which is the dominant approach, is an increasingly risky approach to the concept. Technocrats do not have a monopoly on analysis in an increasingly skilled world. In many fields, officials find it hard or even impossible to keep up with what is going on in science, finance, medicine, even social networking. The idea that experts and elite decision-makers in a few select places can impose their will seems a strategy vulnerable to attack and decay. Crises are nothing new in our world. In previous crises, people turned to states and elite officials. It still may be the case that state and suprastate institutions have capacities that other institutions do not possess. But what has changed is the audience. People are more educated and skilled than they were and less willing to accept authority if they know that the alleged experts have no exclusive grasp on the problems.

Subject to attack as undemocratic and as ill prepared to deal with a globalizing world posing new challenges, it seems likely that this notion of global governance will come under further attack in future years. For many, it remains an attractive way of thinking about how global governance works, especially if they think global problems are debated, investigated and resolved exclusively through elite fora far away from popular input. Whether this is how global politics will evolve remains to be seen.

Scenarios

In the following hypothetical vignettes, our two families, the Masons and the Patels, interpret five key issues within a global governance worldview derived from Institutionalism.

Global financial crisis The great disruption that began in US financial markets in the summer of 2007, perhaps the most significant non-military event since World War II, is a major challenge to ideas about, and implementation of, global governance. This development threatens to change the lives of both the Masons and the Patels in ways we can only imagine. Because of their location on Long Island, the Masons viewed Wall Street with the same mix of awe and contempt with which they viewed the city of New York itself. John, being a vintner, or wine-maker, was dubious about people who 'make money out of money', or, as he sometimes put it, 'make money out of nothing'. His wife, Helen, an elementary-school teacher, found the complexity of stocks and bonds confusing but fascinating. Children Henry and Sofia were not really aware of the financial markets until that summer. They rapidly became aware though, and developed strong views about them quickly.

After the last boom in information technology stocks broke in 2001, the US Federal Reserve system – the US central bank – reduced interest rates to avoid a deep recession (Hall 2008). This made the cost of borrowing money much cheaper, allowing John to borrow for new plant and equipment at his winery. But the low return on this money made bankers look for ways of boosting their yield. This hunt for yield led them to do two things. The first was to invest in emerging markets like India and other countries in Asia. But, more significantly, it led them to become very interested in innovative financial instruments in Europe and America, which offered higher returns than those they were used to in the recent past. When we think of bankers lending money, we think of bank loans, which are paid back over time. This is how John's company borrowed money from the bank. But bankers have created all sorts of ways to buy and sell loans like John's, and mort-gage payments, and those for credit card debt and car loans. Bankers have turned this debt, which is fixed as far as the original borrower is concerned, into bonds called 'structured bonds' that they can trade amongst themselves.

Before the global financial crisis began, the most significant market in these structured bonds was based on mortgages lent to homeowners with relatively poor credit – people with low-income jobs, a history of unemployment and some failure to repay debt on time. These were the so-called 'sub-prime' borrowers. The Masons were not sub-prime borrowers. They had been careful with money and had never been unemployed for long periods. They lived in an affluent area. But, close by, there were subdivisions with modest homes, many of which had been financed through sub-prime lending. Many of the Masons' friends blamed these people for the financial crisis, suggesting they were bad risks and should not have been lent money in the first place.

The Masons' kitchen-table talk reflected their exasperation with the crisis. Their initial reaction to the situation was to see it as a problem that would quickly be solved. They assumed their government would deal with the issue, like John's car mechanic dealt with his fast and rare 1992 SAAB 900 Carlsson he had imported directly from Sweden, when it had problems: find the problem, replace parts and fine-tune. Problem solved. The family argued about who should be blamed, what rules should be changed and how the government could get the economy moving again. Although the problem seemed home-grown, the Masons did see value in their government talking to other governments to get the problem solved. The problems with these bankers were international, they were all interconnected and things did not seem to be solvable just in America. The issue was global. The solution would, at least in part, have to be global too. But they were confident a solution would be found. It was a glitch, and nothing more.

The Patels were initially indifferent to the financial crisis. This was an American problem, asserted Agastya, and they would have to deal with it. How could these American banks have lent money so foolishly, he wondered? The talk on local TV and radio in Bangalore was that India, China and other emerging-market countries in Asia were no longer so closely tied to America and Europe, and did not have to worry if the rich countries had economic problems. Unfortunately for the Patels, this proved not to be so. The world was evidently more tightly integrated and interdependent than they imagined. As the financial crisis affected the purchasing decisions of US corporations and those in Europe, the software companies Mr Patel's small firm worked for suffered. These firms started to lay off workers and sought to reduce their expenses. One of the first things they did was try to cut costs in office cleaning. Mr Patel found he was being asked to reduce his prices even though he had contracts agreed at higher rates. Mr Patel had no choice but to agree if he was to stay in business. But these cuts affected the hours and pay of the people who cleaned for his company.

Now when the Patels talked about the global financial crisis or economic conditions, they were far from indifferent. Agastya and Bhadraa were disappointed that what they had been told proved incorrect. They were more anxious than ever about their situation and the prospects for their children.

If America and Europe fell into a real economic depression, they might have to return to their village, and that would mean a very meagre existence indeed. They thought they were past this and that education and science meant these sorts of crises were a thing of the past. They could not understand how this could happen in the modern world of 'India Shining'. It made them lose some confidence in their political leaders and the value of democracy itself. What they wanted, more than anything, was a quick fix to the problem so they could get back to how things were before 2007.

Climate change   The Patel family had, like most citizens of developing nations, been eager to see development in their country, to advance their nation and themselves. Getting what the West has was what this was all about. When he thought of the environment at all, Agastya pictured the fields he tended in his home village and the fickleness of the weather: good conditions one year, and drought or flood the next. Indeed, drought was one of the reasons he had sought a new life in Bangalore. He was greatly annoyed by western concerns with global warming. It was as if these people had never lived with a harsh environment and did not know how to make do when things were bad. On the other hand, he did not want to make things worse than they need be. He wanted a solution that would allow India to grow at high rates and, if possible, make the world a better place. This meant better technology, such as cleaning products that were non-toxic. But he was reluctant to give up the things he had worked so hard for, such as the air conditioner in his home or the modest car he could now afford. The children were learning a little about climate change in school these days, and they were starting to suggest recycling of household products and ways of cutting down waste. But they were still new to a middle-class life in India, and they wanted all the things children had in affluent countries. So, like their parents, Aditi, Vinod, Janna and Mira were really only willing to make minor adjustments to their lifestyle, and who can blame them?

It was quite a different story in the Mason household. The status-quo arguments about climate change that suggested it could be handled by innovation had, even amongst the technocrats, been largely defeated. More extensive change would be necessary than a faith in technology or short-term fixes could provide. Because John's work was dependent on climate he was acutely sensitive to the issue and an enthusiast for a more intensive response to climate change. He knew that climate is something that does not respect borders, so in family discussions he was always suggesting the value of cooperation between countries in dealing with the issue. Given this, he was frustrated by the record of US policy on the matter and eager to see more global solutions. If John was an enthusiast, it would be fair to say that the Mason children were fanatical about the issue. They had both become censorious of their parents as far as environmental matters were concerned. Henry, for example, took his father's love of his old Swedish car to task, because the car was a high polluter compared to modern vehicles. John responded that, although the car was inefficient by contemporary standards, much of the pollution created by automobiles was produced in their manufacture. By keeping an old, classic car in daily use, he was effectively reusing it and delaying the manufacture of a new one. Although much of the focus on climate change in the Mason family is on practical responses the family can implement, there is an awareness of the global context of the issue. Partly this is a result of the history of US Government hesitancy on the matter. Partly it has resulted from the plethora of scientific evidence and popular documentation of the problem through the media.

Development The Patels, like most other middle-class families in the developing world, are aware of and have strong views on the global order, how it came to be the way it is and what should be done about it. They are acutely aware of the global (and local) divide between rich and poor and are determined that India will – given time – develop out of the poor camp. Agastya has great faith in education and the acquisition of knowledge. Development is simply a technical issue for him, and once it is understood, it can be achieved. India, like China, now seems to understand how to produce development and so they are making their way into the rich world. However, this technocratic vision of overcoming obstacles is tempered by a highly political understanding of the world order in which rich nations are thought to be determined to secure their control over resources and markets. This meant a lot of family conversations had a conspiratorial tone to them, at least from a developed-country perspective.

Things were quite different on Long Island. Like a lot of people in their rich and very large country, John and Helen had grown up with a largely inward, domestic focus. What was happening in the world was of less interest to them than what the US was doing in the world. This reflected an order in which, despite the struggle in Vietnam and inflation in the 1960s and 1970s, the US was the most successful country and the global leader in so many ways. The end of the Cold War magnified this self-confidence, as had success in the two great wars of the twentieth century. But things changed a great deal after the invasion of Iraq. The self-satisfied feeling no longer existed. Like a good number of Americans, John and Helen responded to these changes by becoming more curious about the world and more determined to understand the nature of the world system that was emerging. This was much more the case with their children, who were learning about globalization in school. Rather than taking global inequalities to be a natural phenomenon as their parents had for much of their lives, Henry and Sofia asked why it was that the great disparities in wealth existed and why even finding good drinking water was a struggle in some places. Although they knew things, even water, were not free, they were unwilling to accept things as they were. They wanted change, and in civics classes Henry wrote papers on the need for development and how states could cooperate to make it happen. Sofia too was an enthusiast. The fatalism of the older generation about the world was not shared by the young.

Security   For the last few years, at least until the financial crisis began, security issues, especially terrorism, had been a major issue amongst middle-class families in America, as was also the case, but with less intensity, in Europe. Both John and Helen had vague memories of the Vietnam War – photos of tanks on the covers of newspapers and magazines day after day and the sense of impotent failure it brought to American life in the 1970s. John joined the Reserve Officers' Training Corps (ROTC) in college, and his National Guard unit was activated during the first Gulf War of 1991, although his brigade did not fight in Operation Desert Storm. They both remembered 11 September 2001 vividly. Although it was not their first memory of terrorism – they remembered the Palestinian plane hijackings of the 1970s that led to aviation security screening – it was the first time Americans saw terrorism in the US. John knew this actually wasn't the first occurrence in America, recalling the Weathermen bombing campaign of the early 1970s and the long history of American political violence, including the failed bombing of the J. P. Morgan & Company bank at 23 Wall Street on 16 September 1920. There is no gainsaying the impact of 9/11 on American life and attitudes to the world. Most of the Masons' neighbours were traumatized to varying degrees. Most wanted some form of immediate response by way of revenge. Flying the flag at half-mast was standard throughout their suburb, and pick-up trucks came to be festooned with flags. Gas stations seemed to have more and bigger flags than ever, which is saying something given how enormous flags often are at these American highway stops. The children, much younger then, came home with talk of war on their lips, and family discussions revolved around the question of how to find Osama bin Laden and his henchmen. The rapid invasion and conquest of Afghanistan was cathartic, but frustrating in that it failed to find the alleged culprit until 2 May 2011, almost ten years after the event. The family were split over the mounting focus on Iraq. John recalled the coalition that had supported US action to liberate Kuwait in 1991. As it became obvious that no similarly large coalition was going to form in 2003, he wondered about the motivations for war. While many of his friends and neighbours were happy to 'get' Saddam Hussein, he could not help but think about what regime change would achieve. What purpose would it serve?, he asked. Could the US really change the nature of the Middle East by democratizing through force? John wondered whether a more proportionate and collective response to security threats would be better.

The Patel family, like other Indian families, was familiar with domestic terrorism. They put great store in the Indian armed forces and their ability to respond to these threats.

Although India was a non-aligned country in the Cold War, buying munitions from East and West, ethnic and geo-political tensions in the region had been significant since partition in 1947 created the separate countries of India and Pakistan (and eventually Bangladesh) out of former British India. Pakistan and India had fought a series of minor but bloody conflicts since then. The adult Patels had witnessed communal violence in their home rural area too. Security issues were frequently discussed in school and so Aditi, Vinod and the twins were acutely aware of India's security issues, 9/11 and the 'global war on terror'. Their teachers and their schoolmates mostly opposed unilateral American action, the Iraq War and the detention of 'illegal combatants', as they were called, without a civil trial. They tended to favour intervention in Afghanistan though, and were suspicious of Pakistan. Although the Patel family were aware that the Indian Government had created India's nuclear arsenal in the face of global opposition, they took the view that the United Nations should have had the last word on Iraq's nuclear experiments and thus US failure to obtain agreement on armed enforcement of UN sanctions should have terminated any US initiative. Once the invasion was underway, the Patels read of the disintegration of the Iraqi army with disbelief. Initially anyway, the effectiveness of US military force was very obvious. The 'shock and awe' of the invasion affected them as much as those meant to be on the receiving end. However, as time went by and the civilian casualties mounted, as no evidence of Weapons of Mass Destruction (WMDs) was found, and as accounts of prisoner abuse emerged at Abu Ghraib prison in Baghdad, the Patels and their neighbours, like people all over the world, became increasingly angry and hostile to US military action, believing it to be inspired by more than defence concerns. It seemed to Bhadraa in particular that the US had simply gone too far in invading Iraq after the action in Afghanistan, had defied collective world opinion and were now messing up the occupation and transition from one-party rule to democracy.

Gender relations   The Masons lived lives that acknowledged an equal contribution from John and Helen, although it was clear that John was the major earner. They and their children were dubious about the much more limited roles assigned to women in traditional cultures, especially in developing countries. Although not describing themselves as Feminists, they took the equal rights of women to be normal and right. When they thought about the UN or US foreign aid, they very much expected this to promote the rights of women, even if this meant change to traditional cultures. They were astonished to see that the US invasion of Iraq had seemingly greatly reinforced traditional gender roles. This made them sceptical about the idea of humanitarian intervention in the cause of human rights (Barnett and Weiss 2008).

Things were not so very different with the Patels. Women in India had long had assertive movements promoting their rights and interests. Although Bhadraa looked like a traditional Hindu mother, she volunteered for an AIDS charity once a week, and was determined her female children would be well educated and secure highly paid jobs. While the Patels saw basic equality as normal and just, they were sceptical about efforts by foreigners to remake traditional cultures. They thought this wrong in principle, but also doomed to fail because it tended to underestimate the vibrancy of local norms.

Problems to consider

In thinking about and discussing Institutionalism as a view of global governance, you might distinguish the world of policy-making and implementation from the scholarly debate, and consider the degree to which they seem to share common views, and the degree of their divergence. A second problem you might discuss is the interests of organizations themselves and the degree to which these obstruct a focus on global governance. Last, you could debate the question of whether Institutionalism, coming as it does out of the Liberal tradition, neglects the issue of distributional effects or relative gains of global governance in its focus on absolute gains. If this is so, what are the implications of neglecting the issue of distribution? Does it fatally weaken the case for Institutionalism?

Further reading

A good place to start is Cox and Jacobson's *The Anatomy of Influence* (1973), which contains a series of essays on decision-making in international institutions. Keohane's *After Hegemony* (1984) sets out his research programme on cooperation, influencing a whole generation of scholars who followed in his footsteps. Weiss's views on the UN system and what to do about it can be obtained from his *What's Wrong with the United Nations and How to Fix It* (2012). For work in the constructivist tradition, focusing on the organizations at the centre of global governance, see especially Barnett and Finnemore, *Rules for the World* (2004), which provides a sustained discussion of the problem and will repay careful study. Also see Avant, Finnemore and Sell (eds.), *Who Governs the Globe?* (2010).

4
Transnationalism

Transnationalism is my name for a way of understanding global governance that focuses not on international institutions or national states themselves, but on other agents and processes that complement Institutionalism. In this sense, the focus of Transnationalism is not so much on the basic causes or features of global governance, as on intervening variables that affect or modify global governance. Influenced by Liberal international relations theory and constructivism, Transnationalism is driven by a sense that the mainstream story about international relations which focuses on relations between states does not capture all of what is going on in the world even when it gives attention to international institutions (Risse-Kappen 1995). Perhaps just as important for many is a concern that global governance as conceived by Institutionalism marginalizes large numbers of people, especially the poor and those with no voice who seemingly have little capacity to shape global governance, despite the many problems they need to overcome. For these people, Transnationalism suggests there is another global political process taking place not purely dominated by elites, which might be available to mass participation. On agency, Transnationalism has some common ground with Cosmopolitanism, Hegemonism and Feminism.

This sense that Transnationalism, as I call it, is a force for good should not obscure the intellectual cogency of this approach. The Transnational way of thinking about global governance offers a vital and dynamic view of globalization and its effects; it suggests that international relations is not simply a field of domination but that concerns and interests of large numbers of people can find a voice in global civil society, in NGOs and in global social movements. As a view of global governance, it is easy to say that it does not focus on the commanding heights and is therefore trivial, but implicit in Transnationalism is a view of the changing political efficacy of mass publics that seems to make more sense as we move further into the twenty-first century.

Background

Social movements concerned with issues including the environment, peace and anti-nuclear issues, poverty, famine and challenging the apartheid system in South Africa became increasingly prominent in the late 1960s and early 1970s (although Oxfam was actually founded in the early 1940s). For a generation that came to maturity after World War II, these issues motivated their political activism. This was a time of considerable prosperity in the West as rebuilding after the war had stimulated productivity growth and the rise of a mass production – mass consumption system that provided full employment. This lessened the constraints of scarcity and enabled a shift from an emphasis on relative to one on absolute gains, raising the popularity of free trade. A major feature of the 1950s and 1960s was the beginning of the end of the colonial world as countries in Africa and Asia gained their freedom. But with this change came many problems as large parts of these regions suffered from famine and malnutrition. In the 1970s and more recently, social movements, operating through NGOs, have sought to address many of the inequities produced by the global trade and financial system, by standing up for the rights and interests of people in developing countries and for the global biosphere. Since the end of the Cold War, many countries that had been locked into dictatorship and supported by the West against the Soviet Union have shifted to democratic systems. In this environment, human rights has become a major concern, stimulating widespread activism in the developed and developing worlds.

One of the challenges for those interested in understanding the role of social movements and other transnational agents in world politics is that none of the established theories of international relations took these forces seriously, for decades. Even path-breaking work that professed to be focused on transnational issues, such as that of Keohane and Nye (1977), did not consider social movements or what Keck and Sikkink call 'advocacy networks' (1998). The origins of this problem lie in the rise of Neorealism advocated by Kenneth Waltz (1979). Waltz suggested that international politics was governed by a lack of overarching authority, or what he called the condition of anarchy, which made states unitary actors and meant other possible actors were only of marginal interest. This intervention triggered a fierce debate, with much of the Liberal school eventually capitulating to the notion that anarchy was crucial and that the system was therefore more state-centric than they had previously considered. Ideas were relegated to a residual variable, there to explain what could not otherwise be explained (Goldstein and Keohane 1993). But far from ending the debate about which actors were relevant to world politics, these debates helped promote the rise of the constructivist approach to world politics, which was influenced by a broader range of social theory and was more inclined to accept a larger set of consequential actors, such as social movements and NGOs.

Purpose

Transnationalism encompasses a mix of more empirical social scientists who want to identify neglected agents in world politics, more activist scholars who want to encourage this means of making change, as well as activists more generally in the developed and developing world. The self-concept of all these individuals is that Transnationalism, whether conceived in terms of advocacy networks, civil society or social movements, is a force for the good. This self-understanding can place Transnationalism in either the problem-solving or critical camps, based on Cox's notion of different purposes. Schechter has suggested that a distinct policy-relevant critical theory can be identified (Schechter 1999: 247). The practical engagement this implies fits much of Transnationalism well.

An issue in understanding the purpose of Transnationalism is that it is not clear whether insurgent and 'bad forces' such as terrorism fit into the worldview of this conception of global governance. Although terrorists are certainly most unlikely to be well received by the scholars and activists of Transnationalism, who detest their methods, a case can be made that they share common ground as far as their effort to transform the global status quo is concerned. Given this, groups who cooperate across borders and use illegal and violent means to pursue their agenda should be thought of, however repugnantly, as a regrettable and marginal part of Transnationalism. However, in recognizing that their methods are so much at odds with the rest of Transnationalism, and with other approaches to global governance, it might be more appropriate to consider them further in more specific work on terrorism and challenges to world order.

Puzzles

Implicit in Transnationalism is the view that what was once ephemeral in terms of political change can now, in the different circumstances created by globalization, be highly consequential. In these new circumstances, information flows are greatly enhanced and transparency or awareness about what states do and the implications of their policy choices for their domestic community is much greater than it was in the world of Bretton Woods. But how advocacy networks, global social movements and NGOs actually become consequential, and what they can achieve, are far less clear. This is the ground upon which the puzzles that drive Transnationalism have been generated.

The first puzzle has to do with norms, which have an important place in the analytics of Transnationalism. This shows that Transnationalism is very much an outgrowth of the tradition of Liberal and idealist thinking that permeates the study of international relations, despite the dominance of Realist thought in the security world. This puzzle assumes governments want to be seen to be adopting widely accepted norms. Global social movements and global civil society more broadly somehow transmit new or changed norms to the decision-making institutions. The second puzzle revolves around the process of insertion of what political science would consider relatively weak institutions (and their ideas) into the policy process at the global level. Given the high politics that has traditionally tended to dominate international institutions, how is it that the non-sovereign entities associated with Transnationalism obtain influence?

Level of analysis and actors

Transnationalism adds to the levels of analysis in Institutionalism. For Institutionalism, the key issue is the sovereign state and interaction via international institutions. International institutions matter, but as an outgrowth of states. Determinations about what happens in the world are not as simple for Transnationalism. There are several levels of analysis here. The domestic or local level is crucial, because this is where concerns about health, welfare and how societies are governed are generated. So, unlike in Institutionalism, what goes on below the level of the state is important (della Porta et al. 2006). Above the state are linkages between civil society, social movements and NGOs. This is where transnational communication occurs. It is also where domestic forces bypass their own unresponsive state and seek allies in other states and in international institutions, indirectly applying pressure on their state for recognition of rights and attention to problems. This is the 'boomerang pattern' identified by Keck and Sikkink (1998: 13). This seems to be a complex view of how global governance occurs, across three different levels. But a key role is still assumed by states in Transnationalism. This complex view of global governance may recognize more agents and interesting capacities to affect change in the face of resistant states, but it nevertheless acknowledges that states and international institutions like the IMF, World

Bank and WTO are crucial. So the units involved remain quite tangible. This is an approach free of unspecified forces and processes.

Relevant actors include local, domestic NGOs and transnational NGOs like Oxfam and Greenpeace. The links between these two levels are important politically as this is where local concerns can overcome lack of domestic political support. An important element of this relationship is that transnational NGOs are esteemed agents. These actors typically possess issue-area-relevant expertise and have some international prestige. In a sense they are carriers of international best practice and they use this status to gain influence with governments, and, where necessary, shame them into action. States remain relevant actors in Transnationalism, but states are not the same actors they are in Realist-inspired thinking. States are worried about their reputations here and are eager to adopt international norms. Very few states are willing to ignore international standards and become 'rogue states' like North Korea. What motivates states and what they will respond to are quite distinctive. Other relevant actors include epistemic communities, such as, for example, groups of climate scientists who wish to influence policy by engaging in international debate and advocacy. Again their expertise is highly pertinent in terms of their political salience. Civil society and – at the transnational level – global civil society encompass groups who express their interests and views by association outside the confines of the state (Scholte 2011). Civil society is typically highly developed in the rich world but much less so in the developing world. Transnationalism is concerned with how political association of this sort develops, made up of advocacy groups or what others call global social movements, concerned with political change such as ending gender discrimination and gaining fair access to resources.

Assumptions

Transnationalism assumes the existence of a transnational level of global life which is populated by international institutions and other newer transnational entities, such as global social movements and NGOs (which may be one and the same). Indeed, for many exponents of Transnationalism, a proto-global civil society is in formation, where concerns about global problems are formulated and expressed. States remain very important in this world, partly as an obstacle to change and partly as a target for influence, as in Keck and Sikkink's boomerang model.

Building on neo-liberal institutional ideas about regimes and Rosenau's concept of governance without government is core to this conception of the institutional world supporting global governance. Implicit here is the idea that a better world can be built below and above the state, a world not compromised as states are by their relations. This new world of global governance will be more responsive to social movements and thus more legitimate and effective.

Although there are many frustrations in dealing with international institutions such as the IMF and World Bank, good things can be achieved through them. Global governance as we experience it is not a conspiracy and it can be improved and made more legitimate. Transnationalism is therefore a positive and optimistic account of the potential of global governance.

Despite the idealism of Transnationalism, there is a strong pragmatic element in this worldview. It focuses on concrete mechanisms of governance. It begins with very basic concerns about how contemporary global politics works, or fails to. It is concerned with making small changes and incremental improvement. Transnationalism rejects broad sweeping narratives of change.

Transnationalism has some difficulty with 'bad' movements, such as global terror networks, because of this positive outlook. The approach assumes demand is for progressive rather than regressive change. Was Osama bin Laden really a norm entrepreneur, albeit one with a very different agenda from most considered by the Transnational approach to global governance?

Transnationals assume the new world of global governance is good for groups who want change. But Transnationalism says little about the capacity of states and international institutions to respond to these demands.

An idea that seems to underpin Transnationalism is that transnational actors, networks and the boomerang effect are relatively new phenomena in world politics. This newness offers hope of change. But the newness of transnational processes is less clear. Anti-Slavery International, a contemporary organization dedicated to the elimination of slavery, has its origins in earlier abolitionist organizations in the 1820s. Activism directed against slavery was widespread until the Civil War ended in the United States in 1865. Despite this, the assumption of newness provides some verve and a sense of momentum to the approach.

Most transnationals assume their objectives are inherently democratic. For a critical view, see Scholte (2011). Because they are agitating for those who cannot speak for themselves – in the case, say, of advocates of land tenure reform – the assumption seems to be that this approach to global governance expands democratic choice and should be viewed as extending the scope of an egalitarian society.

Ontology

Transnationalism has an interesting view of what matters in global governance. In focusing below the state, it suggests domestic activist organizations are relevant to global governance. This opens up the ontology of global governance to local and small-scale groups that would barely be considered by other worldviews. Above the state, the focus is on transnational networks that incorporate these local movements. How these transnational networks are organized and how they interact with states and formal international institutions such as the IMF, World Bank and WTO are of great concern in Transnationalism. States, of course, are of concern too, but they are not the primary focus.

Within this system of local and transnational forces trying to bring about change, the focus is on communication of local concerns and demands, and their transformation into global norms for states and international institutions. So this is not an institutional approach as such, because the key things that matter are ideas about policy and the acceptance of these norms by policy-makers.

Legitimacy or the lack of legitimacy is a major focus of Transnationalism. Are institutions that make policy thought to be doing so on a consensual basis, or are they coercive? Transnationals look closely at the political basis for policy, assessing its viability in these terms. For them, good policy is legitimate policy and bad policy is opposed by key actors in global civil society. Alternative structures such as the World Social Forum are considered relevant if they can develop more legitimate policy choices than mainstream institutions.

Implications

An implication of the Transnational approach to global governance is the appreciation of a much wider set of institutions, processes and people than that found in the state-centric and elite vision of Institutionalism. This is certainly a less coherent account, but founded on the implicit idea that the coherence or parsimony of the Institutional approach to global governance comes with a price. The problem with parsimony analytically is that it assumes wider politics do not matter to policy. Normatively, given that adherents to Transnationalism want change in the interests of the marginalized, an elite-driven agenda may not deliver. So Transnationalism is about the process in the first instance, more than it is about the expert-defined objective. Understanding the ways in which norms are diffused via non-state networks and how these come to have significant influence over state policy and the outputs of international institutions follows from the view that ideas matter. One way to interpret this is that Transnationalism is simply taking the global governance system at its word that the outputs of the IMF and World Bank, for instance, are for the wider good. By offering a more fully rounded view of the distributional effects of policy, Transnationalism ensures better policy. Without taking this into account policy will simply fail, suggests Transnationalism.

Unlike the endogenous account of institutions given in chapter 3, the Transnational account of how global governance works suggests an exogenous view in which forces outside the established institutions make these organizations change. It refocuses our attention away from institutions themselves to the wider political processes within which the institutions operate.

Applications

Apartheid was a system of racial segregation and political domination in South Africa. Although segregation on the basis of race had its origins in the initial white colonization of Cape Colony in southern Africa, apartheid was implemented as government policy by the ruling National Party from 1948 until 1994, when white minority rule ended with a new constitution and election of Nelson Mandela as President of the Republic. Jobs, living areas and public facilities were divided up on the basis of race during the apartheid era. Four races were identified under South African law during these times: Whites, Coloured, Asians and Africans (i.e. Blacks).

As you might imagine, thinking about this many years later after this racial system is long gone, organizing politics, housing, jobs and almost everything else on the basis of racial classification was regarded by many people in South Africa and outside as abhorrent. From the 1950s opposition to this domestic policy was expressed by other states. From the 1960s onwards, this accelerated as European colonies in Africa gained their freedom and confronted the white-dominated country to their south with growing hostility.

Intriguingly, by the mid-1980s, opposition to apartheid had become near-universal and a broad sanctions regime was in place, with considerable support from laws passed by the US Congress. As Klotz argues in her seminal work on transnational mobilization against apartheid South Africa, this consensus on opposing South African domestic policy was not something readily explicable in dominant Realist conceptions of international relations theory (Klotz 1995).

Klotz shows how loose opposition to racial discrimination in South Africa was mobilized over two decades. Governments, NGOs and individuals came to agree that what was going on in South Africa was unacceptable. She argues that, from as early as the mid-1960s, there was a 'global norm of racial equality' in the world (Klotz 1995: 6). South Africa was in gross violation of this norm. She goes on to suggest that Realist arguments about national interests (and Marxist arguments about material incentives) ignored the effects of norms. Norms are vital because norms actually change interests. They do this because Realism and Marxism ignore the broader social basis of interests and incentives. These are defined not only in brute material terms but in broader social and political terms that are just as real and immediate (Klotz 1995: 11).

As the norm of racial equality became more and more universal and racist arguments became illegitimate, NGOs, the EU and the (former British) Commonwealth of Nations were able to push states, especially the US and Britain, to adopt sanctions. So change came from the bottom up, but was supported by what had become a vital and unquestionable 'global constitutive norm' as Klotz puts it (Klotz 1995: 165). So what we have here is a dynamic of global governance premised on transnational forces in coalition against a state, making use of a norm to which there was no reasoned response. Not only do global social movements like the anti-apartheid movement matter in world politics, when allied to new universally adopted thinking they can become very powerful forces of progressive global governance.

Differences of emphasis within Transnationalism

The dominant tendency in this literature is the work on advocacy networks by Keck and Sikkink (1998). They find linkages between civil society, social movements and NGOs above states, across the globe. These links enable domestic forces to bypass their own unresponsive state and seek allies in other states and in international institutions. External forces can be recruited for local political contests. The other major tendency in this literature is represented by the work of Rosenau (1992), who focused on the changing capacities of individuals and the ineffectiveness of states actually to govern in a context of global change. Institutions that could offer effective rule in this context would displace states. Individuals have a greater role in Rosenau's schema, as does expertise. In some respects it seems to represent a technocratic impulse, an anti-politics almost directly opposed to the highly political world explored in the findings of Keck and Sikkink.

Strengths

A major strength of this conception of global governance is that Transnationalism challenges the established state-centric view of global governance implicit in Institutionalism, making Transnationalism more flexible in an era of globalization. Transnationalism is not just concerned with states but instead drives the analysis below the level of the state to civil society, including social movements and NGOs. This is matched above the state by the networking of these groups across the globe. So what makes global governance is not just the actions or inactions of states but the work of relatively humble organizations. Global governance is not just an elite phenomenon.

A further strength of Transnationalism is the wide scope of the approach. Transnationalism is willing to look at more levels of analysis and a wider array of actors. It is also open to phenomena in a wide range of issue areas. Global governance is not confined to the high politics of security or even human rights, but is also about health, the environment, fishing rights and aboriginal land tenure, amongst other things. This range of phenomena thought relevant to global governance in the Transnational conception gives this way of thinking about global governance a comprehensiveness not matched by other approaches.

The third strength of Transnationalism is its openness to explanations for global governance developments, such as the end of the apartheid regime in South Africa, that challenge purely interest-based or rationalist explanations that are derived from Realist and Marxist theories. Given that states remain key actors in Transnationalism, how is it that states change in response to transnational activism? The answer seems to be that states are not driven by purely material incentives but have a strong interest in their reputations. In this context, abiding by the emergent norms of global governance is of vital importance to them.

Weaknesses

One of the key principles of rationalist social science is parsimony: the ability to explain a lot (of behaviour) with very little in the way of theory or specification of causal mechanisms. But the analytics of Transnationalism emerges out of a frustration with parsimony and a determination to embrace a wider set of causes. Although attractive to adherents in the academic world and to non-academics, this relevance does exclude the large academic audience with a firm base in parsimony. It also makes the basis for the explanation of global governance outcomes much more complex than in Institutionalism, making causation harder to decipher, and it puts a premium on strong field research.

Given the complexity of explanation in Transnationalism, we do have to ask where power resides in this approach. As I discussed in chapter 2, Barnett and Duvall's (2005: 46) 'productive power' acknowledges the effect of power in shaping the identities of the parties involved, disciplining them, making them into what they become. So Transnationalism does acknowledge power in this specific way as we saw in the Klotz discussion of apartheid, but it is also light on simpler relational or behavioural conceptions of power, in which A gets B to do what B would not otherwise do. It is harder to see these direct forms of power being played out in Transnationalism.

The emphasis on doing good in Transnationalism is admirable and a major reason the approach has strong support as an approach to global governance. But what about 'bad forces'? It seems odd that Transnationalism does not put emphasis on movements and illicit NGOs that want to break the current global order not for a wider, more inclusive order, but – at least on most reasonable readings – to create a less enlightened, less open global system founded perhaps on specific interpretations of sacred texts or on traditional cultural norms. Not dealing with the bad movements means that the analysis of these groups and their relationship to global governance is left to those with traditional assumptions about the primacy of the national state and with perhaps less appreciation of the ideas that led to this illicit form of resistance to the global order.

Likely future development

So how will Transnationalism develop as a conception of global governance in the years to come? An area where thinking is likely to develop is in relation to the 'bad guys' (Mittelman 2010). Why, as Frieden, Lake and Schultz ask, do some transnational networks resort to violence when most do not (2010: 382)? Research has suggested a number of strategies, as identified by Frieden, Lake and Schultz (2010: 393). Work in this area may radically transform Transnationalism's conception of global governance, as the potential for non-progressive outcomes receives more attention than it has up to this point. This will make Transnationalism quite different from how it is now.

Following their success in creating and using global constitutive norms to achieve change, activists are likely to try and deploy these to shame governments into action more in future. Given this and the desire of some countries to continue with traditions such as eating whale meat in Japan, we are likely to see states develop more anti-social movement strategies to combat transnational forces. In this world, security and defence will be defined not purely in terms of traditional military resources, but in terms of combating protest and civil disobedience from civil society. Attacks on social networking systems may be a key step in this direction.

We still do not know how norms become global and how they come to have a constitutive effect, in the sense of defining the possible rules of the game in an issue area such as the environment or women's rights. Further research on these ideas, starting with John Searle's thinking, seems likely to be useful (Searle 2005). How do norms arise, grow and get communicated across the world? What makes norms change into other norms? How do norms come to have the power to influence states into conformity? Why are some norms more successful than others?

Overall comments

Transnationalism is a positive conception of global governance. It suggests that improving the world is possible and developing the means of global governance can be done. We cannot eliminate capitalism or the state system, but we can make things much better, not just in aggregate terms, but in a liberally distributed way. Although there are differences within Transnationalism, the approach seeks ambitious levels of change within the norms of the existing state system. This approach is not as revolutionary as might first appear. It is fundamentally a reformist way of thinking about global governance.

By contrast to Institutionalism, we find in Transnationalism a highly inclusive approach to how global governance is understood to work. While elites, in the form of elected and appointed officials, have important roles in states and international institutions, Transnationalism's emphasis on governance above and below the state means that this conception of global governance is dependent on greater political participation. This participation may make action harder but it also gives the results much greater cogency.

Transnationalism is a highly political approach. While all ways of thinking about global governance are political, this is often unacknowledged. In the case of Institutionalism, for example, the emphasis is on technocracy and expertise, and the denial of politics is pervasive. With Transnationalism, politics is conceived as a positive resource in the development of effective and legitimate global governance, so politics is encouraged rather than submerged.

An intriguing part of this embrace of politics is much greater attention to the role of ideas and norms. Institutionalism focuses on material incentives and sees ideas as effect rather than cause, and therefore of little real interest. But as the apartheid case demonstrates, ideas and norms can have real and significant effects on governance. Rather than being ephemeral, ideas and norms, when held intersubjectively – that is, between people – can have powerful effects. People come to consider such norms to be facts, like other facts about the social world upon which they base their actions, such as the state. Although the state is often presented as a material thing, it is really no more than an intersubjective idea which is vulnerable to collapse, as illustrated by the events of 1989 and the Arab spring. This internalizing of norms and their status as what John Searle calls 'social facts' is a tremendously powerful focus of Transnationalism, both analytically and in terms of a target for political action.

The tone of Transnationalism is highly practical. Unlike some other ways of thinking about global governance, which can be rather abstract, this conception puts emphasis on concrete policy and governance issues to do with real-world matters of energy, resources, gender equality and making international institutions work better. Although practical, it is not clear how effective this approach to global governance could be in dealing with crisis. While communication and agreement are key to dealing with global crises such as the financial crisis that began in 2007, so is executive action.

Scenarios

Our two families – the American Masons and the Indian Patels – have hypothetically embraced the ideas of Transnationalism and interpret five key issues within this global governance worldview.

Global financial crisis   John and Helen Mason were astonished by the events surrounding the global financial crisis that began in 2007. John had invested some of his pension fund with Lehman Brothers so was very disturbed to see the firm go into bankruptcy in late 2008. John and Helen found themselves talking a lot to their neighbours about these issues. The Masons had always been concerned that capitalism was not well regulated, especially in America. They had memories of grandparents who told stories about the Great Depression of the 1930s. Their connection to the land made them somewhat dubious about the games played on Wall Street too. Their neighbours, some of whom were quite prosperous, were very agitated by these events. John and Helen saw a change in these people, many of whom started to talk about the need for markets to work for people and not against them. Many were especially concerned about the vast size of the bail-out funds made available to keep the banks in business after Lehman failed. Many of their cherished assumptions about savings and investments were being seriously challenged in the younger generation too. Henry and Sofia, always quite independently minded, were shocked by the financial meltdown. Like most modern American teenagers they had been exposed to a lot of talk about money and how good it is to have lots of it. Popular culture reinforced these ideas. Henry found himself drawn to activism, after trawling the internet for others who shared his views about the need for protest and change. He was determined to participate in local efforts to provide social housing, and to find out how people in other countries were reacting to the crisis.

The Patel family was unusually active in local social movements. This could be attributed in part to Bhadraa's background. Her mother had been very involved in fighting for land tenure reform in the Indian countryside before the family came to Bangalore. Bhadraa viewed the events on Wall Street as a part of a much deeper problem with capitalism, in which ordinary people do not get a voice. More recently, Bhadraa's activism had focused on debt relief for highly indebted countries and on highlighting what she saw as the problems with IMF and World Bank policy. Agastya, although very busy with his business, took the view that finance was like a casino and kept away from it, apart from his efforts to save money.

Although not as radical as his wife, Agastya had long been concerned about debt and these events made him more focused on doing something about his concerns and supporting his spouse. The children, although not allowed to participate in civil society campaigns, were well aware of the issues, and these were discussed in the family. Like the Masons, the events in the rich countries reinforced their belief that it is necessary to stand up and protest against bad things. They appreciated the wide-ranging scope of the crisis in the West, and that many parts of society were hurt.

Climate change   Problems at the winery had caused John to step outside of his usual comfort zone and get involved with local Long Island campaigners for carbon emission reductions. This made John something of a radical in his town, but he felt sufficiently strongly that it made sense to pursue the matter. Increasing temperature and rainfall were affecting the water table under his vineyards. He could see the change from year to year. Pretty soon he knew the area would be too damp for grapes as they would suffer from disease and parasite attack. Starting out small, John began with letter-writing campaigns lobbying Albany and Congress in Washington for policy change. John enjoyed this and found others looked to him for leadership. After being involved with this for a while, John found himself in Copenhagen for the climate change conference. John, now thoroughly immersed in the science and policy of climate change, was deeply disappointed in the results of this meeting. He would have to try harder and push governments to get change.

Henry and Sofia Mason, like others of their generation, were very familiar with climate change. For them it was simply a fact with which they had to deal. But, unlike some others, they were not fatalistic. Something could and should be done to address the problem. But they watched their father and came to the conclusion that shaming governments into acting was crucial. Going around states, influencing others to think differently about climate change, and making changes locally seemed possible. They sought change at school and at home, saving money for the school district and for the family by using less energy and by reusing products they used to throw away. They faced some opposition to this at school where a lot of their peers were happy little consumers. Keeping at it, talking about the science and what would happen without change, brought results. While plenty of teenagers would not care, the brighter ones could see the problem and being aware of climate change started to become fashionable. It became common-sense amongst their group, and it was increasingly hard for the school to ignore their view that change had to occur in how the school did things.

Climate change had long been visible in Bangalore, with wetter rainy seasons and hotter summers. The Patels were worried about conditions for their rural relatives and about life in the city too. They increasingly were starting to believe that the national Government of India was too reluctant to act on this matter and needed to be pushed, even if this meant from outside India. They wanted growth and improvement in living standards, yes, but not if it meant climatic disaster. Although not actively involved in activism in this area, the family did hear about the activities of others they knew, who were involved in NGOs devoted to climate change. Although not rich, the family were willing to provide some money to these groups so that they could continue their work. The family discussed doing more and they started to give recycling and reusing of products more attention. When talking to their friends, they noticed a small shift in the ideas people had about climate change. It was not just a problem for the West any more. That would probably mean action in the years ahead.

Development The Patel family had been interested in development for years and often had discussions of the problems that were thought to hinder it. Both Agastya and Bhadraa read about the issue in newspapers and magazines and watched documentaries on television about development in India. The notion of development had been part of the currency of ideas in their community since they were children. It was part of the national consciousness of being Indian and it mixed with memories of malnutrition and famine from earlier times. So the motivation and emotion attached to development as an objective were very tangible. In recent years, the debate between the adults in the household had changed. In earlier years, the assumption was that development was natural and inevitable. But Agastya and Bhadraa had become much more politically informed in recent times and they no longer viewed development like this. As they saw it, it was not inevitable that the benefits of growth would be enjoyed by everyone. While they were happy to get their share like others, they thought that it was entirely conceivable India could grow fast and the benefits could be enjoyed by just a few. They thought this could and should be avoided and saw it as a practical task to organize at the local level, ally with foreign non-governmental agencies and pressure their own government into changing its thinking about development so that a more horizontal model was put in place. This would make development more legitimate, effective and sustainable.

The Masons were practical people too, but they knew the first step to changing the world was changing how people think about the world. Once you have done that, people will feel that things are different and they will act differently. As a wine-maker, John felt a special affinity with the idea of development, as it implied to him an organic process of growing and enhancing the world, which he did with his grapes. John had clearly never looked at any steel mills in the developing world! Much of the action on development in the family revolved around Henry. Henry was a thoughtful fellow, a little different from his peers. He felt a sense of empathy with people in far-off places and saw development as the key to a just and more effective world. He did not view this in vague cultural terms though. For him, as for the Patels, development was about practical politics. Henry's particular concern was reforming America's protectionist agricultural policies. Over eighty years or more, these had helped create an unreal rural world in much of America, while at the same time driving up the cost of living for working people (the American 'middle class') and denying people in the developing world markets for their produce. Henry joined an activist group devoted to reform of these inequities by pressuring the US Government not directly, but via foreign powers. The logic here was to expose the hypocrisy of America's talk about free trade and practice of protectionism. Henry hoped the group he was in could build enough momentum, in association with others, to shame the US Government into policy change.

Security John and Helen Mason were conscious of some of the ways the issue of security had been used by western governments since the tragedy of 9/11. The Masons were quite cynical about this. They could see that the encouragement of fear kept people in line and quiet. When 9/11 happened, John was attending a workshop on new viticulture techniques in California. After phoning home and making sure everyone was OK, he spent a lot of time, as people did all over America and all over the world, talking to his colleagues about the events and what they meant. Fierce displays of patriotism were quite unexceptional at this time, but that is not how John's fellow workshop participants behaved. Many asked how the United States had caused these terrible events to transpire and what it is the United States could do to mend relations with the rest of the world. This reaction, which was mirrored on some college campuses across the US, was not the dominant reaction. But it certainly left its mark on John who returned home, after a very long rental car drive from California, thinking about what should be done to undermine the hostility to the United States in some parts of the developing world. John had been in the Peace Corps as a young man and he decided to get involved again in volunteer activity abroad, in order to show others that Americans were not all the 'crusaders' of terrorist propaganda. With his developed agricultural skills, his services were in demand in South Asia and Africa. It was just a matter of persuading his family and his boss to let him go for a time.

The Patels were disturbed by 9/11 like the Masons, and like John Mason there was some interest in being involved in work that would undermine the basis of terror. The Patels were one of those Indian families who were divided among themselves by the division of India and Pakistan in 1947. Some of the family remained in what became Pakistan. This had, over the years, led to much stress as the relationship between India and Pakistan went through many periods of strain and some of war. Despite these problems, the older Patels had stayed in touch with their cousins across the border even after they moved far south to the Bangalore area in the

1960s. Agastya and Bhadraa, although much younger, still valued these connections and kept them up with phone calls and email. This personal link made the adults in the family eager to see peace in their region and willing to get involved in civil society links between Pakistan and India. In this sense the family were participants in a transnational dialogue between the two countries that went above and below the state level. The Patels also participated in efforts to influence Indian policy toward Pakistan, based on the premise of common interest and similar identity. The familial links gave this political work a real meaning to the adults in the family. Their sense that politics can be changed, that even global governance is subject to action from below, was acute.

Gender relations   The practical theme also translated into the Masons' view of gender relations. The family had, as a result of an initiative by Helen, had a discussion of domestic tasks. Everyone accepted that they had something to contribute and they did – although whoever said it was easy to motivate teenagers to do their chores? Helen still ended up with the responsibility for things, which annoyed her at times, although it did mean she had things just as she liked them. Helen too was the prime mover as far as thinking and acting on gender relations as an issue of global governance was concerned. Helen had long been concerned about the trafficking of women for the purposes of prostitution and she was interested in how women in developing countries, and in particular in places like Afghanistan and Iraq, were treated. Being an active person, she would attend lectures on women's issues at the famous 92nd Street Y in New York City, taking the Long Island Railroad to Penn Station. The 92nd Street Y was a place of social activism, and Helen became involved with organizations such as the National Organization for Women, which linked up with non-American organizations to pressure for women-friendly public policy and cultural change around the world, often lobbying UN-linked organizations. Although she thought of herself as a non-political person, this work on lobbying and activism started to get her interested in formal politics and she eventually joined the political action committee of a local candidate for elected office in county government.

Although Bangalore is a relatively modern and progressive place, traditional attitudes to women persist in many quarters. This was annoying for the Patels. They had left the countryside and were very much in favour of modern ways of doing things. They liked their culture but some aspects of it belonged in the past, just as they do in all cultures. The parents recognized that education was key to driving out old ways of thinking and putting in place more appropriate ideas. So they encouraged their female children as much as they did the boys. Evidence of sexism at school was grounds for complaint and this extended to bullying. Bhadraa, although no longer a rural dweller, still had strong emotional ties to this world. For her it was essential to transform how women were treated in the countryside too. This led Bhadraa to become involved in a group that advocated the rights of women and children through activism and links to international NGOs. In addition, Bhadraa found herself periodically travelling with other women to conduct regular clinics in rural villages. These clinics might involve a talk, a play of some sort, a discussion with the audience of relevant issues and ways of addressing them, and usually some sort of subsdized giveaway, such as cleaning products or food. This was not always well received and even Agastya found it hard to understand at times. But this sort of direct action mobilized Bhadraa and it made her activism directed at politics more focused.

Problems to consider

In examining Transnationalism and global governance, you might want to discuss the following. First, is global governance a substitute for inadequate or malevolent states? What does the 'boomerang model' say about the changing effectiveness of global governance? Second, you might discuss norms and the power they can acquire as intersubjectively held expectations. Where do global constitutive norms come from, and what are the circumstances that make them more likely to be successful? Are they always benign? Is it possible to think about norms that some states would want to resist, such as consumerism? Last, you should discuss the 'bad guys'.

Why do a small number of transnational groups resort to violence? Does bringing violence into Transnationalism force us to change this concept of global governance? If so, how?

Further reading

The literature on advocacy networks is fascinating. The reader should read all of Keck and Sikkink, *Activists Beyond Borders* (1998), for a start. Klotz's *Norms in International Relations: The Struggle against Apartheid* (1995) and Della Porta et al., *Globalization from Below: Transnational Activists and Protest Networks* (2006), also show what this tradition can do very well. Thomas Risse's collection, *Bringing Transnational Relations Back In: Non-State Actors, Domestic Structures and International Institutions* (1995), is an important and useful survey. The reader should immerse themselves in Rosenau's discussion of global governance. A great place to start is his essay in Rosenau and Czempiel (eds.) *Governance without Government: Order and Change in World Politics* (1992). The reader should then consult his *Turbulence in World Politics* (1990), *Along the Domestic–Foreign Frontier* (1997) and *Distant Proximities* (2003), amongst several other volumes.

5
Cosmopolitanism

Global governance was, as we have seen in chapter 3, conceived as a practical problem by Institutionalism. For technocrats, global governance is about managing the problems thrown up by a globalizing world, largely through the traditional means of intergovernmental organizations. Although global governance has its origins in these important pragmatic concerns, the idea has been attractive to others with different agendas.

Cosmopolitans are an important group of theorists interested in global governance. They take a much broader and more optimistic stance on global governance compared to Institutionalism and the Transnationalism considered in the previous chapter, looking at its potential for human development and progress. This account of global governance is more concerned with the potential for the reform of institutions and human relations, and Cosmopolitans are less willing to accept a limited problem-solving view of what global governance can achieve. This provides common ground with Hegemonism and Feminism, discussed in chapters 6 and 7 of this book.

This wider view of what global governance is and what it should be challenges the idea that concepts should be limited to analysis of the world. Although concepts are always likely to be statements about how a thinker or a like-minded group want something to be, at least implicitly, these normative commitments are often hidden behind a lot of social-scientific preamble. Cosmopolitans are typically social scientists, but their commitments are not hidden. Indeed, their desire to transform things is explicit and gives their discussions of global governance an excitement and relevance attractive to many.

If the watchword of Institutionalism is 'continuity', then that of Cosmopolitanism must be 'change'. Unlike many trained in international relations theory, Cosmopolitans do not start with a world of sovereign states in an unchanging vacuum of anarchy. The very environment in which global governance is taking place is changing, in the Cosmopolitan view. Mainly based in universities, think tanks and philanthropic institutions, these analysts take a more systematic view of the response to globalization, suggesting that substantial modifications to existing governance systems are necessary, given the change to our world. Informing their analysis are strong normative commitments to deeply held values associated with individual liberty, democratic representation, equality and social justice on a world scale.

Background

Thinking about a fairer and more just world has a long tradition in modern thought, which we can trace to thinkers such as Rousseau and Marx. In the twentieth century, the most radical strand of thought associated with this tradition inspired revolutions in several countries, including Russia and China. However, a more accommodating, reformist wing of this school of thought eschewed revolution and sought to reform and revitalize capitalism and western democracy from within. Putting emphasis on the universal rights of all citizens, equal opportunities for the disadvantaged, and the need for capitalism to tame the worst abuses of the work process, the reformist or social democratic tradition sought active engagement with electoral politics so as to further its cause. Labour and social democratic parties have been major features of the electoral landscape in most developed countries since then.

As with Institutionalism, we can trace the origins of Cosmopolitanism in part to debates in international relations theory. The dominant thread in that debate is Realism, which takes the interest in survival of sovereign states operating in what international relations scholars call anarchy – an international system with no overarching authority – as the system's organizing principle. Countering Realism was the Idealist or Liberal tradition which saw the states as having strong interests in cooperation. This interest in cooperation was potentially transformative. While not being able to do away with anarchy, Liberals thought the public goods like free trade, a stable currency and collective security that could be generated from cooperation were at least as likely to be enticing to states as the more cautious stance suggested by Realism. Where Realists always looked at the relative position of their own state versus others, and were therefore always focused on the relative gains from any negotiation, Liberals were more concerned with aggregate welfare, and so absolute gains were the issue for them. All can gain from interaction, even if some gain more than others. We can live with some measure of inequality as long as we all make progress. Cosmopolitanism picks up on the mutual benefits from cooperation, the attraction of absolute gains, and the concern with values and norms that the Liberal worldview enables.

Global change provides the immediate stimulus for this approach to global governance. The reformist tradition was successful in helping to create a post-World War II order in which a measure of social security was provided in the developed world. The Depression of the 1930s, the alternative order represented by the actually existing socialist world and post-war productivity growth were the immediate causes for this success. But from the late 1960s onwards, productivity growth lagged, and by the 1980s new liberalizing governments in America and Britain sought to restructure markets and the social security systems that surrounded them, exposing workers to greater individual risk. The Cosmopolitan approach is in part a response to this change, seeking a new sustainable model. Although this background is important, more recently Cosmopolitanism has also been motivated by a wider range of concerns. The rise of identity politics such as sexual preference has been important, as has the recognition of the significance of multiculturalism.

Purpose

In contrast to Institutionalism, there is a grander vision of change implicit in the Cosmopolitan concept of global governance. What seems to drive these reformists is a concern that global change is both encouraging the idea that democratic choice is legitimate and should be available increasingly to all, and at the same time actually constraining the choices available to national governments as the pressures of globalization hinder their local policy autonomy (Held 1995: 21). It is as if a buffet of menu options is available to all, but nobody can afford the increasingly steep price of the meal. In this context, global governance is seen as an important means through which change, which seems to just happen to us, can be adapted to human purposes. It is only through global governance that the human population can effectively tackle these global forces, which increasingly are too big for national governments.

An effective way to understand this approach is to think of markets and how they work. Markets for goods and capital (money or finance) operate within rules or regulations. This is so that they are fair and monopolists, for example, cannot exploit their position and charge exorbitant prices. Regulation can also address potential conflicts of interest when a bank gives advice to a customer on where to save their money. In this example, the bank may not otherwise offer the best advice but only highlight products offered by the bank. Regulation may also try to stop the unscrupulous, such as bad car dealers who might try to sell defective cars to people who do not know how cars work. Here the issue is lack of information and preserving the public good of safety. Globalization offers benefits in terms of variety and price of goods and all manner of interactions. Like domestic markets, this is attractive to most people. However, just as markets do not work as we would always wish them to, it is the same with global change. Globalization, while adding richness to our lives, may also outsource our job, bring large-scale migration and give rise to mass urbanization such as in coastal China. Global governance in this context can serve to modify change so that it meets human needs, provides for collective welfare and does not undermine the commitment to liberty and free interaction. The purpose is a critical one – to transform the status quo – but it is a limited critical purpose, in that the target for adaptation is not globalization, which is thought to be effectively unstoppable, but rather the global governance mechanisms that deal with the consequences of globalization. So, rather than transforming the fundamentals of the social world, as Cox suggests is the purpose of critical theory, Schechter identifies a policy-relevant critical theory (Schechter 1999: 247). It is this more amenable purpose which fits the reformist Cosmopolitan vision of global governance.

Puzzles

Cosmopolitans assume understanding the world is intellectually demanding and that very basic questions about the structure and functioning of the global system are worth asking. They hold fewer fixed axioms than the technocrats of Institutionalism, and are thus open to a wider range of more penetrating questions.

The Cosmopolitans conceive of globalization as a social phenomenon, but not subject to easy human direction or control (Koenig-Archibugi 2003: 7–9). Like environmental problems, economic and political change at the macro level is complex, involving many different systems. This generates policy problems of unprecedented difficulty (Whitman 2005: 59).

The key puzzle posed by the Cosmopolitans has two elements. The first is analytical. Given that the likely causes of so many of the challenges faced by the world's population are not confined within national borders, what is the correct means to tackle these problems? Given the global nature of these problems, purely national solutions are likely to be inadequate.

The second element focuses on the character of an effective response. The Cosmopolitans are concerned with the sets of ideas, norms and practices which support social solidarity, rights, social justice and democracy (Held 2006: 159). Once these concerns are addressed, it will be possible to design new systems of global governance that address complexity and change via more legitimate and sustainable means. Without legitimacy and sustainability, it is likely that efforts to tackle global problems will fail, suggest the Cosmopolitans.

Given the above, the drive amongst Cosmopolitans is toward the development of global governance which not only solves 'technical' problems, but addresses more hotly contested problems of political alienation, and social and economic inequalities. But it is important to understand that for the Cosmopolitans these dimensions to a solution are not just add-on options. They are fundamental to the success of any global governance strategy.

Level of analysis and actors

Cosmopolitans have become interested in global governance because the concept helps them address the authority shifts that have been so characteristic of the world since the end of the Bretton Woods era in the 1970s. For many traditional international relations scholars, such as the Realists, only states really matter in world politics because there is no over-arching authority above states. This makes states self-regarding and the key actor. But outside the field of international relations (and amongst non-Realist thinkers within the field), this view of an unchanging world of states is not so easily accepted. Cosmopolitans embrace a much wider view of what are relevant phenomena than do Realists. Many different forms of human association are potentially relevant, including businesses and social movements.

Global governance allows for the possibility of solutions outside the straitjacket of the sovereign state. Unlike Institutionalism, which looks 'up' to intergovernmental organization for global governance, the Cosmopolitans have to consider a variety of levels for sources of such governance. A purely international and institutional analysis does not capture the range and depth of global governance in their analysis.

Unsurprisingly, governments at all levels, local, national and international, feature as major actors in the Cosmopolitan conception of global governance. Although the Cosmopolitans respect expertise and the application of science, like Institutionalists, they have a much greater appreciation of the role of politics in the success of policy. Global governance is not just about finding out what the right answer is. The right answer may well involve the acceptance of that answer amongst many different groups of people. So here politics is not a negative interfering phenomenon, as it is in Institutionalism. It is an essential resource for effective global governance.

As a result, Cosmopolitans embrace civil society actors like Amnesty International, Oxfam and Friends of the Earth. Civil society is important because Cosmopolitans are more modest about the possible achievements of governments than they once were, and they recognize that other forms of authority and capability are characteristic of the age of globalization. Cosmopolitans also recognize the vital role civil society institutions can play in promoting and legitimizing global governance solutions to pressing cross-border problems.

Cosmopolitans are also attentive to the existence of international business. Capitalism, understood as a distinct, historical system of social relations, has a persistent, vital place in the Cosmopolitan worldview. So, it is not surprising that, for the Cosmopolitans, any conception of global governance must include global businesses as key actors.

Assumptions

Cosmopolitanism, like most political traditions, looks to state institutions first. But, unlike in Institutionalism, there is not the same assumption that global governance is by definition an elite process. Although elites are certainly involved in leadership roles, the assumption here is that global governance only really works when it has a substantial political base outside the elite.

Global governance is clearly a much bigger and more important concept in the Cosmopolitan worldview than it is for the technocrats of Institutionalism. Cosmopolitans do not think they can change the fundamental processes that produce problems. But they can change the mechanisms we have to deal with problems.

Cosmopolitans assume that normative concerns such as justice and fairness are central to global governance, and that the point of making change is to make the world a better, fairer, more just place. Not only is the normative element desirable – what we want from global governance – it is also essential to the effectiveness of global governance.

Like the technocrats, the Cosmopolitans assume science and expert knowledge to be at the heart of global governance. However, unlike in Institutionalism, the Cosmopolitans appreciate that political issues such as legitimacy and distributional effects are necessary and appropriate parts of the decision-making process (Dryzek 2010). Without these, in their view, global governance will not work.

Unlike the technocrats of Institutionalism, who are strongly influenced by neo-liberal thought, the Cosmopolitans see institutions and their uneven impact on specific groups as key to making global governance work. The Cosmopolitans take a more solidaristic approach to governance and to the development of society, in which social protection is a valued component.

Politics is understood as an ever-present element of social life and therefore part and parcel of global governance too. Unlike Institutionalism, which treats politics as analogous to corruption, politics is understood by Cosmopolitans as a system-reinforcing phenomenon.

Ontology

As is the case with Institutionalism, government is clearly privileged in this understanding of global governance. None of the ways of thinking about global governance examined in this book can afford to ignore government. But, unlike the technocrats of Institutionalism, Cosmopolitans do not over-privilege government as they think is the case with Institutionalism. Because of their analysis of globalization, they understand authority relations are changing and that an effective global governance analysis will be based on a wider set of actors than just government.

As is the case in Institutionalism, it is clear that the Cosmopolitan conception of global governance places great emphasis on knowledge as a source of authority. Many of the primary developers of this conception of global governance are professors. This means that an understanding of global governance will focus on knowledge producers and the processes through which knowledge is created.

Political representation is important to Cosmopolitans, given their origins and the critical role of legitimacy and consultation in their thinking about global governance. Elective politics is a key part of global governance and needs to be considered closely.

Cosmopolitans share with technocrats an interest in law, education and the development of human capital. In addition, because politics has such a central role in their understanding of global governance, the media have an important role in the spread of ideas and the generation of support.

Implications

The Cosmopolitan conception of global governance is a positive and optimistic view of how the world and its institutions can be changed for the good of all. This conception of global governance is premised on confidence that wide and deep change is possible and likely. Although a much broader and less practical approach, the Cosmopolitan conception offers a brighter and better future. Because of this, Cosmopolitanism is an attractive and potentially popular conception of global rule, which should appeal to a much broader audience than the narrowly elite conception offered by Institutionalism. It offers more to a larger set of people.

Given this, political mobilization around Cosmopolitan ideas needs to be considered seriously. As I noted at the start of the chapter, the sort of ideas that form the background for this thinking have motivated political parties for more than a century, and these parties have changed domestic policy greatly in developed countries, introducing workplace laws, minimum wages and a whole raft of welfare legislation. One implication of Cosmopolitanism at the global level might be developments of this sort, creating a social safety net, but at the global level. A development like this would pose a major challenge to modern capitalism, used as it is to moving around the globe to secure the greatest advantage to itself in terms of costs.

This very popularity may raise problems. Inevitably, a key feature of global governance is the rule it provides. An approach such as this one that places emphasis on consultation and representation may pose problems for the generation of rule. This poses a risk of incoherence and immobilization. As a minimum, global governance must provide governance.

In principle, this approach offers a real challenge to the tradition of state sovereignty the world has been familiar with since the Peace of Westphalia in 1648. By bringing in a whole series of new actors, it promises to rewrite the rules about what matters in international relations. Central to this challenge is the role of new agents in world politics, such as NGOs and global business. Institutionalism tends to discount these new forces but Cosmopolitanism takes them seriously. They are understood as disruptive and able to bring about both positive and negative consequences for humanity. It is up to us to make sure, via global governance, that the positive outweigh the negative. Lacking any deep sense of the dynamics that produce these phenomena, Cosmopolitanism tends to see globalization as a natural process to which we have to adapt.

Applications

The major place you will find expression of this conception of global governance is in the views of NGOs, especially those with interests in the developing world. It is fair to say that the emphasis on knowledge, the legitimate role of politics and the importance of fairness and global justice is almost the common-sense of our age as far as civil society organizations are concerned. In as far as the United Nations' Millennium Development Goals (MDGs) place emphasis on gender equality (MDG 3), we can also find some evidence of the application of Cosmopolitan principles inside intergovernmental organizations as well.

Outside these venues, the best place to identify Cosmopolitan influence on global governance, or at least global governance debates, is in social democratic parties, especially in Europe, but also in parts of the developing world. The search for a 'third way' between neo-liberal market capitalism and the state capitalism of actually existing socialist regimes of the past has been the context in which concerns about global governance have been articulated (Giddens 1998).

Differences of emphasis within Cosmopolitanism

Cosmopolitanism has a long tradition of thinking going back to antiquity and, more recently, the work of Kant. In the discussion of global governance, however, Cosmopolitanism has been dominated by the thinking of David Held and his co-authors, especially Mathias Koenig-Archibugi. For the Cosmopolitans, globalization brings benefits but also costs. Given the global nature of these costs and benefits, purely national solutions are not going to be adequate. How to respond? The Cosmopolitans want to develop the ideas, norms and practices which support social solidarity, rights, social justice and democracy in the context of global change (Held 2006). The strategy then is a compensatory one, which recognizes what Institutionalism does not, which is that globalization has distributional effects. In order to sustain the good things about globalization, we need a system of global governance which compensates for the bad, such as the outsourcing of work which tends to hit lower-income communities hardest.

Strengths

The Cosmopolitan conception of global governance is very attractive as a way of thinking about a desirable world, for three reasons. This approach recognizes change and the necessity to reconfigure global governance in order to accommodate new global threats that cross borders, and new agents of authority. Global governance is not simply another term for international organization, but an understanding that globalization has changed the basis for global cooperation and altered the capacity of states to act independently.

A second strength of this conception of global governance lies in its recognition of the valid role of politics in global cooperation. The Cosmopolitan conception is a politically informed view. Recognizing the legitimate role of politics, rather than labelling politics as a form of corruption, makes the approach much more accurate as an understanding of how global governance operates.

The emphasis on a normatively desirable world, in which global justice and fairness are concrete goals, is a considerable strength as it makes this way of thinking about global governance enormously popular with people who are otherwise disenchanted with politics (Hay 2007). Not only does the Cosmopolitan conception of global governance promise a better world, it suggests that, without its emphasis on justice and fairness, the world will never solve the looming global challenges of the twenty-first century. This provides a rational basis for a very strong commitment to the idea of a more equitable global system.

Weaknesses

The Cosmopolitan conception of global governance is not without its problems. The fact that most of the proponents of this way of thinking about the world and its challenges are observers outside the practical world of policy and implementation inevitably robs this conception of some of its power. There is the risk that this conception of global governance will be dismissed as speculation.

The emphasis on politics at the heart of this conception is a weakness as well as a strength. One of the characteristics of our world is the equation of politics with all things corrupt. By embracing politics, Cosmopolitans may be acknowledging the reality that politics matters, but may at the same time taint their conception of global governance for some groups, especially perhaps the technocrats who would be charged with implementing such a global governance strategy.

Inevitably, the normative quality of the conception makes the Cosmopolitan idea of global governance vulnerable to criticism that it lacks realism and practical salience, and that the ideas about a better world get in the way of practical plans for making the world we live in function better.

Likely future development

The Cosmopolitan appropriation of global governance is relatively new. In the absence of future great-power war or major wars with middle-powers (with Iran, say, over nuclear weapons and regional ambitions), and assuming a United States chastened after the costs of the Iraq occupation and the war in Afghanistan, the prospects for this conception of global governance seem good. Talk is cheap, certainly compared to dropping guided munitions, especially in a time of fiscal crisis. International cooperation is one of the quiet success stories of globalization, and despite much rhetoric, states have many interests in pursuing cooperation. This is especially so given the cross-border character of many challenges today: climate change, financial instability and crisis, terrorism and migration. The arguments for reducing inequalities and furthering global justice are perhaps a harder sell, especially if this suggests new taxes on those in the rich countries. Much will depend on the effectiveness of more coercive approaches to global problems. If these prove overly costly or unsuccessful, the Cosmopolitan approach to global governance might well emerge as an increasingly practical and successful conception.

How might Cosmopolitan conceptions of global governance develop in future? The protective features of Cosmopolitan thinking about global governance seem ripe for development in a world where the perception of threats from crises is heightened in the wake of security concerns over terrorism and frustrating failures of economic and financial systems. Cosmopolitanism's ideas about making global change work for all seem attractive in these conditions. Cosmopolitanism will not want to banish globalization, seeing this as a positive force bringing opportunity to previously neglected parts of the globe, but will, following Polanyi, want to make sure globalization is embedded in sufficient social protection to make it seem equitable and sustainable (Polanyi 1957 [1944]).

The more accommodating elements of Cosmopolitan thinking may find it attractive to abandon the more explicit political qualities of this approach to global interaction. Many Cosmopolitan thinkers, like those with other views, are involved in pragmatic policy areas and are drawn toward more problem-solving work. So the effect of crises can go both ways. Some Cosmopolitans will continue to think about major change, while others will be less willing to think in bigger, broader terms.

Overall comments

For both analytical and normative reasons, the Cosmopolitan approach to understanding global governance is an important way of thinking about global change and the challenges it poses. It is an attractive conception of the potential in global human interaction. Cosmopolitanism is both idealistic and hard-headed. It says there is something worth struggling for. The world can be made a better place. Our lot is not to struggle with interminable conflict.

Building on success at the domestic level, the thinkers behind Cosmopolitanism have sought to extend their approach to cross-border problems, based on the understanding that globalization creates many externalities that single states are handicapped in addressing. Globalization is a good thing, suggest Cosmopolitans. It brings us opportunity, knowledge and efficiency. It allows domestic society to question established tyrannies, as in the case of the Arab spring.

But globalization has side-effects such as outsourcing and rampant consumerism, which undercut living standards and job opportunities and create pollution, further global warming and ruinous debt. Cosmopolitanism says these externalities of global change must be internalized so that we can be sure the net effect of globalization is good for the whole world and not just for one or two parts of it.

Unlike some other ways of thinking about global governance, the Cosmopolitan approach is one of responsibility and action. It does not accept that outcomes are natural. Even if there is little we can do to stop globalization, we can shape it and how it affects the poor so that it does not disadvantage them. Moreover, the approach says it would be irresponsible not to intervene to shape globalization. Irresponsibility is morally wrong, but also inefficient, just as it is inefficient to fail to regulate malfunctioning markets.

The future importance of this approach to global governance depends on global geo-political events as well as the veracity of the thinking behind the approach itself. As a highly political approach, it faces considerable opposition from critics based, especially, inside the United States. But it is this political quality that gives this approach its vibrancy and tendency to ask difficult questions which Institutionalism will not ask. This quality gives Cosmopolitanism an enduring appeal to many.

Scenarios

In the following, our two families, the American Masons and the Indian Patels, interpret by means of hypothetical vignettes a set of global governance issues, this time within a broadly Cosmopolitan framework, as established above.

Global financial crisis When John and Helen Mason became aware of the developing financial crisis in 2008 with the problems at Bear Stearns and the freezing of the financial markets they reacted, like most American families, with alarm. They had savings and pension plans in financial institutions and were worried about the safety of these organizations. As events developed they learnt about how global the financial system is, and how vulnerable it is to manias in housing and new financial instruments such as Collateralized Debt Obligations, and, of course, how vulnerable the markets are to panic and collapse too. This certainly was not a world of which the Masons approved. They were hardworking people and although risk was part of life, they did not see it as something to be played with. When the financial markets start to resemble a gambling casino, they reasoned, things were out of hand. While they recognized the value of efficient financial systems if they make your savings work harder for you, they saw this as merely a means to an end and not an end in itself. But the financial market seemed to have become an end in itself. So, like millions of other Americans, and billions of other people around the world, they took the view that it was time for a thorough remake of the financial system to ensure it serves the interests of society, rather than the other way round. They appreciated this would mean the Government would have to take a stronger hand, but they welcomed this after years of being told the markets knew best. Plainly, they didn't. Helen reacted by joining a club in which surplus household items were traded amongst members. As the crisis developed they started to realize how global the markets were and became critical of the US Government's largely domestic economic focus. Much more cooperation was necessary across borders to solve a problem that plainly did not respect national frontiers. But solving this problem was not enough. Global finance had blown its credibility and needed to be remade, and it should not be the bankers or their client politicians who controlled this process.

Aditi Patel wrote a paper on the global financial crisis for her economics class. She, like the rest of her family, were amazed that such a thing could happen in America and then spread to much of the rest of the world. It so contradicted the views her teachers held, which tended to emphasize the self-regulating aspects of markets. If this was self-regulation, she argued, let's have something else entirely. Father Agastya and his wife Bhadraa felt let down by this crisis. These bankers, they were supposed to be so educated and so able.

How could this occur to such people? The older Patels concluded that their trust in these institutions had been misplaced. Bankers would have a lot of work to do to rebuild their reputation. Agastya was very happy his business did not yet involve any major borrowing. However, he was concerned that the downstream consequences of the crisis in terms of jobs lost and businesses failing in the software sector would seriously affect him. In 2009 this proved to be the case, but watching this process unfold reinforced to the Patels how interconnected things are in the global economy and the need for cooperation across borders to deal with these problems. Like the Masons, the Patels were strongly of the view that more than a temporary patch-up to global finance was required. Nothing less than a wholesale restructuring would be sufficient.

Climate change   Global warming had been an issue for some years in John's work. His vineyards were very sensitive to weather, like most crops, and he had noticed that in addition to hotter summers and greater flooding concerns, snow cover was much briefer and patchier, and storms were much more intense. These changes meant more damage from weather events in the short term. In the medium term, it meant he might well have to change the grape varieties he was growing as the established varietals were no longer suitable for the climate. It might even mean in the long run that the North Fork of Long Island was no longer a suitable place to grow grapes. Given the intensity of this problem, John was unwilling to accept quick and simple solutions. He was anxious that the problem be dealt with comprehensively and relentlessly. The graphic nature of the issue and the threat it posed to his livelihood mobilized him, pushing him to change how the family lived. However, his obsession with recycling, which he shared with his children, was very much informed by scientific knowledge rather than faith. This is one of the reasons why he kept his old car. He thought he would produce lower carbon emissions by avoiding the manufacture of a new vehicle. In addition to becoming carbon focused at home, he started to become active within his local growers' association, lobbying the county for policy change and going to the state capital in Albany to talk to the New York state governor about the issue. John, a long-time cynic about politics, had become politicized by climate change. His enthusiasm to pursue change was infectious and soon he had the support of his whole family. The issue, being one that did not respect borders, forced the family to think in terms of international cooperation, but also to support NGOs that pursued the science and the policy of climate change.

The Patels had always been very concerned about justice, fairness and doing the right thing. This ethical sense ran through most aspects of the family's activities. Although the family's livelihood was based on business, Agastya was determined that his company would not be destructive of the lives of his workers or his neighbours. This made him acutely sensitive to some practical issues of water and cleaning-product use. Unlike his competitors, he was determined only to use products that were safe for the environment and his workers, and to minimize his water use. Agastya's wife, Bhadraa, shared his ethical concerns. But she saw these in a wider context and in time became interested in political campaigning. She could see that politicians of the mainstream were unwilling to pursue the climate change issue, but she felt that the science and the uncertain effects of climate change on the world demanded action. She was determined that there should be an effective political process to debate policy responses to these changes, and that things should not be buried in bureaucratic inertia. The children, especially Aditi, were captivated by the issue, and the interconnectedness of different climates quickly gave them a sense of the links between nations and the necessity for cooperative action on the part of governments. Vinod organized a mock United Nations meeting at his school because he shared his sister's views about the globality of the issue. The mock UN debated the issue at length and then issued a resolution mandating the setting of global standards after agreement between rich and poor countries. Far from climate change being an irritating issue of interest only to the rich it was something that all countries had a stake in, thought Vinod.

Development   Helen studied political science in college. From the start, she was interested in why poor countries were poor and in their relations with rich countries. John, whom she met at a local hardware store while he worked part-time as a student, shared her concerns. After college they both joined the Peace Corps and worked in Africa: Helen as a history teacher; John as an agronomist. It was interesting work and deepened their understanding of the issues and their ethical commitments. They had done their best to raise their children with these concerns in mind. Henry and Sofia were unusually aware of the world outside the United States. Henry had just completed three months abroad in Jakarta, Indonesia. Although the children certainly were motivated by what they thought was right, their views on development were as much driven by their keen sense of what is likely to work politically. A sense of injustice, the children seemed to understand, is a barrier to cooperation and prosperity, and so a widespread view that the global order was a just one was essential to progress on development. As a consequence, the family was determined to consume fair-trade products whenever possible, and the children lobbied their school through their student council to do the same. The family took the view that government could do a lot, but that other institutions could make a difference to development too. They were especially interested in debt relief for highly indebted poor countries, and decided to start supporting an NGO that lobbies for debt relief from the World Bank. In addition to recognizing civil society, the Masons were also interested in what business could do for development and often discussed how major American corporations operated and their influence on the lives of people in the developing world.

The adult Patels tended to think of development in very political terms, as a matter of justice. For the adults, how wealth is distributed in the world today reflects what happened in the past. The history of colonialism made India a poor country because, in their view, the colonial power organized things so that wealth flowed out of the country. This being the case, it was important that how the world is organized be changed so that these relationships that create poverty can be brought to an end. So development is not simply a technical issue of how many water pumps you have for a village, it is also about how world trade is organized and which companies dominate particular industries. Their view tends to be characterized by the idea that people have little control over what prices they are paid for their goods and that more control at this level will bring greater prosperity. At the same time, they are aware of the benefits of international cooperation on trade, science and health. Often they talk as if their own government is a major obstacle to development when it is in alliance with foreign companies. Like many other people, they are enthusiasts for micro-finance, especially in the rural areas where their relatives live. Micro-finance loans have helped Agastya's aunt to open a small mobile-phone shop, selling pre-paid phones in an area where the wait for a landline can take years and many bribes. The Patels are vehement critics of the World Bank and IMF, which they see as dominated by western interests. They, like many in developing countries, want voting rights reallocated on the basis of population and away from the size of contribution, as is the case at present. In their view, India and China have made successes of themselves in spite of these institutions and not because of them. What is needed is new governance in these agencies or new institutions altogether.

Security   Although the Masons were deeply shocked and grief-stricken by 9/11 just like other Americans, they took from the event a very different lesson from many others. Rather than seeking to hit back and punish those who had perpetrated this appalling crime, they were eager to understand the motivation that led to this horrific act. Being aware of different cultures and attuned to the foreign policy behaviour of the US and how it is viewed in other places, they tried to understand what must have driven those who planned and executed this terror attack. While initially this approach led to some scepticism and even scorn being directed toward the family, this changed over time as the occupation of Iraq was met with a concerted insurgency. While in no sense apologists for terror, the discussions in the family were always made with a clear awareness that the attacks were not perpetrated by states. This act could not be confused, say, with the German invasion of Poland in 1939. Moreover, sadly, it was clear that the terrorists had support in the developing world and so a strategy that did not address the basis of this support would fail. This attitude to security as a combination of potential force and attitude (or coercion and consent) they also applied to rising states like China and old foes like Russia. In the Masons' view, as summarized for a school project by Sofia, there was nothing inherently bad about Russia that made her an enemy. After all, England had nuclear weapons too. At one time, long before possessing nuclear weapons, England was an enemy of the United States. This being so, how the US dealt with Russia must be key to the development of relations between the two countries.

The Patels were much more used to political violence than the Masons, and lived in a state that had fought a number of minor but bloody border wars since its foundation in 1947. Atrocities like 9/11 had been all too frequent in their recent past, including the Mumbai attacks of 26 November 2008 that took about 164 lives. For many of their compatriots, India's status as a nuclear power was a major achievement forcing other states to acknowledge the country's interests and importance. Yet the Patels' dinner conversation was quite different. The parents stressed the value of knowing the perspective of the other side and the value of the effort to understand and accommodate. Much of this was cultural. Agastya's company employed Indians of different faiths and he was obliged to acknowledge their different habits and practices. Indeed, as his business grew, Agastya made a point of hiring people from the different communities and of avoiding their segregation into different work teams. This did not always go easily and he often met with real opposition in trying to mix these groups. The Patels were proud of their approach and saw it as a reason why Indian democracy had persisted, despite communal clashes over the decades. They took an interest in the festivals of other religions and encouraged their children to view this diversity and mutual tolerance as part of the strength of India. They were not pacifists, by any means. Vinod had expressed an interest in training to become an officer in the Indian army, and Agastya was determined to give him a chance to fulfil his goal. Typically, the Patels much preferred mutual (or multilateral) rather than unilateral approaches to security, and put great faith in the development of regional organizations in South Asia that could work to combat the animosities that developed in the post-colonial period.

Gender relations   For the Masons, gender equality was an assumption and a habit of daily life. Although John made more money than Helen, she also contributed more to the running of the household in many ways, despite his best efforts. Her education made her more aware of the world in some ways than he was with his more vocational background. Helen's mother had been interested in women's liberation in the late 1960s and early 1970s and this was part of the world in which Helen matured. In daily life the Masons did their best to show their children that women were equally valued, and that abuse of women was abhorrent. The equality in their domestic life translated into their views of international relations. They supported human rights as they saw this as a way of improving the lives of women in other societies. They wanted foreign aid to be conditional on equal treatment of women and girls. Although wary of the use of force, they cheered when girls returned to the classroom after the defeat of the Taliban. They were mortified when it seemed the US invasion of Iraq had provided the opportunity for women's rights to be subjugated there. Practically, the Masons showed their support by contributing to an NGO that opposed genital mutilation and supported the rights of girls and women in other societies. An issue which John and Helen debated frequently was how to win legitimacy for women's rights in traditional societies. They realized that without resolving this political issue any gains that might be made in rights for women could easily be undone. Their resolution of this problem was to rely on the effects of prosperity – in other words, like birth control, the rights of women are more likely to be accepted in a society experiencing real growth and improvement in living conditions, especially in conjunction with mass education.

For the Patels, the issue of gender relations and the rights of women was something they knew well. Although not a major activist, Bhadraa did support her local women's rights group through small regular donations, attending meetings and discussing issues with her friends and neighbours. Agastya knew well the views of his wife on this subject. Intellectually, he agreed with her, but because he had been raised in a traditional household he sometimes found her views challenging. But he knew better than to argue with her about these. Although in many ways still a traditional society, India has had an active women's movement for two generations and for educated women it is normal to assert gender equality. Practices in the countryside are often very much at odds with this change, but the Patels had, after all, left the countryside for a new life. Bhadraa checked that her husband did not treat his female employees unfairly, or allow his male workers to mistreat his women staff. In educating the children, equal time and money were spent on the female and male children. Much of this was reinforced in school, where girls were expected to be equal participants in class. Indeed, Aditi had responded brilliantly to this and was the academic star of her family. She wanted to become an engineer or a physician. The Patels wanted international cooperation on improving the rights of women in other countries. Although they were sensitive to cultural issues, they were unwilling to tolerate exploitation and abuse. On this level, although they were generally very much opposed to military force, they were delighted that Afghan girls had the opportunity to return to the classroom after the US invasion and regime change.

Problems to consider

In examining Cosmopolitanism and global governance, you might want to discuss the following. First, how accurate is the view of the costs and benefits of globalization in Cosmopolitanism? Are Cosmopolitans right to think that addressing the distributional issue will compensate for the problems globalization brings for vulnerable parts of national communities? Second, where do national states fit into the Cosmopolitan view of global governance? The approach does not seem to say much about states, but surely they are going to be vital in any system of global governance. Last, is there any substance to Cosmopolitanism? What does it propose for global governance, or are its ideas too unspecific about global power? This last point raises the question of whether Cosmopolitanism is a little too ethereal for something as potentially concrete as global governance. The approach may be long on discussions of ideas but rather short on workable plans that could actually be implemented.

Further reading

For statements on Cosmopolitanism and global governance, read Held, *Democracy and the Global Order: From the Modern State to Cosmopolitan Governance* (1995); Held and Koenig-Archibugi, *Taming Globalization: Frontiers of Governance* (2003); Held, *Global Covenant: The Social Democratic Alternative to the Washington Consensus* (2004); and Held, *Cosmopolitanism: Ideals and Realities* (2010). For a broader appreciation of the issues involved in a Cosmopolitan approach to global governance, you might also read Dryzek, *Foundations and Frontiers of Deliberative Governance* (2010).

6
Hegemonism

Marxism is an approach to understanding the world and an agenda to bring about change to empower the majority of people in society. Marx began with a few key observations. First, labour is reduced to a commodity and labourers must sell their labour to survive with the arrival of capitalism. This was a major change from the feudal world where labour was tied to location. The commoditization of labour made the exploitation of labour invisible as labourers were free to sell their labour to the highest bidder. Second, those who controlled the means of production were the powerful of society. Last, labourers gathered in factories acquired consciousness of their exploitation and looked for ways to break out of their condition. The dominant theme in this analysis is the structure of social relationships and the impact these constraints have on people, organizing them into classes and developing their thinking.

Marxist and Marxist-influenced scholars have been writing about the global order since Karl Marx himself wrote pieces for the *New York Daily Tribune* in the 1850s. Although Marx never produced an analytical treatise on global affairs on a par with *Capital*, writers influenced by Marx and by associated thinkers such as Antonio Gramsci, the Italian socialist, have made substantial contributions to the analysis of world affairs, including imperialism, military conflict, global trade and finance. Much of this work anticipates the working of Liberal and constructivist international relations scholars on ideas. In terms of making change, Hegemonism – the Marxist-derived conception of global governance – shares much with Cosmopolitanism and Feminism, as discussed in chapters 5 and 7 of this book. In this chapter I concentrate my exploration of Hegemonism on the followers of Gramsci, or as they are sometimes known, the *neo-Gramscians*.

The contemporary left critique of global governance does not, like the anti-global-governance thinkers I discuss in chapter 8, reject the concept of global governance altogether. Instead, situating globalization and global governance within the capitalist system, which they understand to be a social mechanism with its own laws of motion that stretch across the planet, the Hegemonists suggest that *actually existing global governance*, as opposed to an ideal of global governance, is very much tied to the prevailing social and economic structures of exploitation and inequality that dominate our world. This gives their analysis of global governance an immediacy and relevance in the face of crises in production, finance and consumption that the other ways of thinking about global governance struggle to match. Although a very grounded approach in this way, the Hegemonist conception of global governance is a very politically focused way of thinking. Thinking through concrete practice is at the heart of this approach.

Background

Marxism is often associated with the state socialist regimes in Russia, China and Eastern and Central Europe. When these regimes ended and China started to pursue a market-driven direction, many people assumed Marxism, like Communism, was also dead. But this assumption never stood up to analysis. While the formerly socialist regimes did use Marx's name and in the early days clearly were very interested in Marx's ideas about the problems of capitalism, this was not true in more recent decades when Marxism became a convenient ideology of opposition to the West and these regimes pursued increasingly tyrannous directions. Marx actually had almost nothing to say about a post-capitalist future, apart from a few lines about diversity of occupations in the *Communist Manifesto*. His life's work was devoted to developing what he considered to be a better-reasoned explanation for capitalism and how it operates at the centre of modern life. Outside the formerly socialist world, another problem in how we have interpreted Marx is the tendency to see his thinking in purely reductive terms, placing emphasis on structure and almost negating agency. But any thorough reading of Marx must include his historical works, in which he brings together his more systematic claims with the variety of political experience. It is this work of historical synthesis which has inspired the contemporary Hegemonism considered in this chapter.

Since the late 1960s, a more open and flexible form of Marxist analysis, loosely motivated by the thinking of Gramsci on the role of ideas, has emerged in the study of international order. This work has been associated with the conceptual writings of Canadian political scientist Robert W. Cox. Cox, a scholar and practitioner of international organization in the 1950s and 1960s, with decades of work in the International Labour Office in Geneva, produced a series of seminal works in the 1980s (Cox 1987; Cox with Sinclair 1996), which inspired a generation of studies of global governance by writers including Stephen Gill (1990), Craig N. Murphy (1994) and Kees van der Pijl (1998).

The innovation in Cox's thought was to relax the narrow conception of material or economic determination falsely attributed to Marx's understanding of capitalism, by introducing ideas and institutions which he suggested should be understood as forms of production themselves. The point of seeing ideas and institutions as features of production is that necessity and struggle over who gets what from production are typical of human history. Cox suggested that whether ideas, institutions or material capabilities were causal in any concrete historical situation was a matter for empirical research, not prior theoretical assumption.

Purpose

Not surprisingly, the agenda of a Coxian or Gramscian conception of global governance is a radical or critical one. Marx and his followers were part of a long tradition of critical reflection on industrialism and urbanization. For Marx, these developments in nineteenth-century Europe stemmed from capitalism, which he understood to organize society as feudalism did in the Middle Ages. Marx thought only labour produced value, and saw capitalism as a mode of production at the centre of which was the exploitation of labour by the owners of the means of production. As workers were gathered in factories they tended to acquire consciousness of their exploitation.

For many people inspired by Marx's writings about capitalism, the agenda is to do something about exploitation. Most narrowly, exploitation occurs because those who produce through their labour only receive a portion of their production in compensation. Marx argues that machines do not produce value but only enable labour to produce more. So, in the Marxist view of things, wage-labour is always exploitation and there can be no such thing as a fair wage if capitalists make profits. These views led to a vibrant analysis of imperialism and colonial expansion into new territory by writers in the first two decades of the twentieth century, including Lenin (1917).

This very specific technical sense of exploitation developed by Marx and his followers is less used today. Most people are more concerned about inequalities rather than the exploitation of labour-power by those who own the means of production. Inequalities refer to the wide gap in earnings between senior managers and shop-floor workers in industrial corporations. Is it fair that some people can earn hundreds of times what others do, for the same hours of work? This broader concern with inequalities rather than exploitation of labour-power has inspired a large body of writing about developing countries and their problems interacting with developed countries on unequal terms. The activities of western multinational corporations, low wages in developing countries, historically low commodity prices, and high debt have all been issues for analysis in this tradition.

Marx did not say much about how politics works in general, despite his many historical studies of specific political episodes, and Marxists have debated the role of the state in the capitalist mode of production ever since he died in 1883. Some Marxists have argued that the state is an instrument of the capitalist class – those who own and control the means of production – while others have suggested the state has some autonomy to organize and restructure capitalism when crises occur. More recently, writers in this tradition have emphasized the many different forms political organization can take in different places because of varying circumstances.

The 'Hegemonists', as I have labelled them, think that understanding the substance of global governance requires analysis of what they term a historical structure, closely associated with the hegemony of the neo-liberal or free-market form of capitalism. Even for scholars like Michael Schechter, and Craig N. Murphy (2005), who have more policy-focused concerns, and who do see positive possibilities in the reform of the institutional arrangements of global governance, there is a strong desire to transform the objectives served by actually existing global governance into those that would serve to raise populations out of marginalization and exploitation, serving basic human needs.

Puzzles

The Gramscians want to know how specific historical systems or structures work, and what potential they have for change and transformation. This means both a static analysis of the links between ideas, institutions and material capabilities, and a dynamic analysis of the problems or sources of tension that might give rise to change. The Bretton Woods monetary order mentioned in chapter 2 is an example of such a historical structure.

Within the context of these historical structures, key questions concern the construction and maintenance of hegemonic blocs of social forces. How these alliances that integrate elites and masses are stitched together is of great concern (Germain 1997). The role of ideas in these processes, and especially the role of intellectual leadership fascinate the Gramscian scholars of global governance. I should stress that the objective is not to develop a simple formula or equation which explains the role of ideas – the Hegemonists are far too sensitive to historical difference to think that possible.

The Gramscians have been especially interested in developing a closely reasoned analysis of the neo-liberal or free-market form of global governance. Their work examines the implications of ostensibly technical institutions and exposes their latent political implications (Sinclair 2005). This concern with critically evaluating technocracy such as that of Institutionalism has driven them toward making knowledge itself a subject of critical appraisal (van der Pijl 1998).

Level of analysis and actors

How broad or how narrow is Hegemonism's thinking about global governance? As we have seen, Marx started with the labour process, and was concerned with the social relationships that underpin industrial production. These relations are regarded by Marxists as the starting point for their analysis of capitalism. It is a distinctive view of where to start an understanding of global governance not shared by other perspectives examined in this book.

The Gramscian approach is centrally concerned with the interplay of ideas, institutions and material capabilities in specific historical combinations. These historical structures rise, interact and fall through time and geographically (Cox 1987). By developing the concept of historical structures, which is clearly a much more complex social system than Marx's mode of production, Cox has tried to distance himself from the rather simplistic interpretations of Marx's analysis provided by many later commentators. Cox is not trying just to depict historical variation though. His historical structures do focus on some things and not on others. Perhaps the best way to think about this is to observe that if Marx undertook the analysis of capitalism, Cox took it as his task to consider the different forms capitalism has taken in different combinations of circumstances.

At first glance it may seem that Cox's thinking operates at a high level, in rather abstract terms. But this would be a misunderstanding. Cox and those influenced by his thinking endeavour to build their understanding from the 'ground up' rather than the 'top down'. Other approaches tend to locate global governance in a separate sphere above the normal work of the world, and even the political sphere. This is not true of Hegemonism, which sees global governance as linked to capitalism and the world of work. Perhaps more than other approaches, the Hegemonists have undertaken serious work on very nitty-gritty institutions and processes through which global governance occurs in the context of capitalism.

This tradition is unusually practical and concrete compared to other approaches to global governance. It has translated into a concern with rules, norms and institutions, of both formal and informal character. Although a focus on institutions is hardly distinctive, Hegemonism does not consider institutions in isolation, as is the case in most other approaches. The key thing is considering rules, norms and institutions in their capitalist context. This implies an understanding of the basis of their interconnection and an appreciation of the variation to be found historically and geographically. Murphy's (1994) work on early international regimes reflects this focus, combining institutional analysis with an appreciation of the broader environment of capitalist development which stimulated demand for international cooperation on rules for shipping, mail and the telegraph.

The Gramscians have focused first and foremost on elite institutions, or what we might call control mechanisms at the commanding heights of society. This institutional approach reflects their inheritance of the concern with forms of state power from earlier Marxist scholarship. More recently, this elite focus has been complemented by research on marginalized peoples and processes in developing countries (Persaud 2001; Murphy 2005). Apart from Cox's early work, and some of the large corpus of more recent work by Murphy, many of the writings by the Gramscians have been concerned with governance within capitalism, rather than the traditional focus on recognizable intergovernmental organizations.

Social forces – including classes defined by their relation to production – and elites – defined by their leadership role in relation to classes – have been major concerns of most of the Gramscians. Like Marx, Cox and his followers have been very concerned with labour and workers, especially in the research of Harrod (1987), Harrod and O'Brien (2002) and Bieler (2006). Unlike most Marxists, Cox has been happy to combine the study of classes and smaller, narrower elite groups. In particular, Cox's notion of a Transnational Managerial Class (TMC) that combines leading corporate executives, politicians, bureaucrats and others, spanning developed and developing countries, has proven of great interest as a way of making sense of the development of neo-liberalism in the 1980s. Cox's notion of a leading elite group owes much to the power elite tradition associated with C. Wright Mills and other critical scholars of American politics and society (1956). For many orthodox Marxists, the TMC is not clearly defined in relation to production. For Cox, it is this complexity which gives the concept its power and relevance.

Assumptions

The Gramscians share adherence to the notion that capitalism is a system of social relations, or a social mechanism, that – like mechanisms in the physical universe – shape human social life. But, like Marx, they strongly affirm that, within the limits set by these mechanisms, life is made by people. Like constructivists, with whom they share many assumptions about the world, the Gramscians accept Marx's view that the historical structures or mechanisms of the social world can be reinforced or undermined by human action (Barnett and Finnemore 2004). But they are very clear that change of this sort is difficult to achieve in immediate political activity. Differences within capitalism are therefore as common as differences between capitalism and other mechanisms.

Although very much concerned with processes of consent generation, the Gramscians assume that power, hierarchy and exclusion are key elements of political life and therefore essential to the study of global governance. Because of this it is easy to conclude that the Gramscian reading of global governance is negative. Global governance seems, in the conception of Hegemonism, to be largely a mechanism of control rather than an agent of freedom, although the most optimistic scholar in this tradition, Craig Murphy, sees more hope in intergovernmental organizations than do other thinkers (Murphy 2005: 11).

Ontology

Because they do not think international cooperation occurs in a vacuum, like others influenced by Marxism, it is fair to say that many of those influenced by the Gramscian tradition look to the subject matter of political economy for the things that matter to them. This means they are interested in major corporations, stock exchanges, the labour process and other features of material production. These material phenomena are crucial because they create many of the problems international cooperation needs to solve. A classic issue, for example, is standards. Standards govern things like the size of nuts and bolts, drain covers and electricity voltage. These rules make the handling of shipping containers the same whether at the port of Aden or Sydney.

But the Gramscians are interested in ideas and their reproduction too. This means both mass-media studies and the understanding of education, expertise and other epistemic producers. Hegemonism also takes seriously collectively held ideas about how the world works, such as norms and practices. Collectively held ideas can be very powerful and closely shape how disparate communities deal with problems. But Hegemonism also recognizes, perhaps to an increasing degree, the significance of culture, and how this shapes human expectations and how ready people are to cooperate between societies.

Many Gramscians see historical structures such as neo-liberal capitalism as their proper subject matter. For them capitalism in general is not the issue. The issue is change and how things like the state, like business, like international cooperation take different forms over time. Within this focus on change, Hegemonism is concerned, amongst other things, with how alliances of social forces between elites and classes can be explained. Intellectuals, understood as providing leadership in the formation of new ways of doing things, are also important in principle, although little substantive research has been undertaken on them by this tradition.

Implications

The Gramscian notion of actually existing global governance, understood primarily as a tool for enforcing neo-liberal capitalism as a hegemonic historical structure, sees global governance as part of the hegemonic arsenal of discipline. Contrary to some of the perspectives examined in this book, the Hegemonists think global governance is not an inherently liberating concept. Indeed, it may simply be a new and more effective approach to generating domination.

Although grounded in a big story about the changing nature and forms of capitalism, one implication of the Gramscian view of global governance is that it moves the focus on global governance away from conventional institutions of international order, toward less visible organizations that have been little considered previously, grounding global governance in a more material and everyday context (Hobson and Seabrooke 2007).

Implicitly, given the Gramscian concern with counter-hegemony, global governance could, in the right circumstances, become the means through which a different and more encompassing historic bloc of social forces might develop. But such a development cannot simply be willed into existence and it is clear that Hegemonism does not provide a cook book for it. This is why change is often surprising, whether it is the end of the Cold War or the Arab spring. Hegemonism insists that we put aside the assumption that the structures and institutions we encounter are immutable.

Applications

Marxist-inspired social analyses used to permeate western social science. In sociology, studies of the working class and the labour process were numerous. Political science also had political economists inspired by the Marxist tradition. A related tradition could even be found in the Economics profession. Until the 1980s this was less true of the study of world politics. Just as Marx started to have less salience in these other social sciences with the end of the Cold War, Hegemonism became more popular in the study of world politics. Perhaps this was because it focused in part on the significance of business, and because the role of ideas was important in Hegemonism.

Academia was not the only significant application. Some of the insights from Gramscianism, and other Marxist-derived views, can be found in different forms in the anti-capitalist protest movements that started to appear in the mid-1990s, most famously represented by the anti-WTO ministerial meeting protests in Seattle in 1999, and by the World Social Forum events that run in competition with the World Economic Forum at Davos, Switzerland, each winter.

In addition, the anti-war movement in the West and a new wave of assertiveness in developing countries in opposition to America's post-September 11 foreign policy looked like unexpected resistance to neo-liberal global governance. The talk associated with these movements seems to be far removed from either a technocratic or Cosmopolitan understanding, and to reject an America-centric understanding of world order. This is reinforced by the rise of China and the sense of relative American decline.

Unlike some other approaches to global governance, the Hegemonists include these mass phenomena in their understanding of what makes up global governance. This is because global governance, in the view of Hegemonists, is not just about what happens in board rooms and VIP lounges. If that were true it would imply a very simple view of politics which neglects the ability of people to respond to things that happen in their lives. Because the theory of politics underpinning this view of global governance includes an anticipation of mass response to elite initiatives, Hegemonism sees global governance and what is associated with it in much broader, fully rounded terms. Perhaps this breadth, which allows for mass influence in certain circumstances, gives the world-view represented by Hegemonism its real power and significance.

Differences of emphasis within Hegemonism

There are two main tendencies within Hegemonism, although they are closely related, and suggesting there are two tendencies should not be read to imply that the people who follow one are in any sense opposed to views of the other. The first reads global governance in terms of the imperatives of global capital (Gill 2008). The second is more open to the possibilities created by the institutions of global governance. This tendency is exemplified by Craig N. Murphy (1994, 2005), who sees positive possibilities in the reform of the institutional arrangements of global governance. He asks how we can transform the objectives served by actually existing global governance into those that would serve the marginalized.

Strengths

A great strength of this conception of global governance is its base in the material life of production, broadly conceived. Unlike some other notions of global governance, which may seem too much like volunteer work or charity, the Gramscian approach sees global governance as a hard-fought and gritty political reality, just like other features of a difficult and con-flictual world. Global governance can often seem to be a world of ideas inhabited by the perpetually optimistic, Pollyanna-like in their hope and faith in a future world of justice and equity for all. Hegemonists do not have time for such nonsense, to their credit.

A second strength of the Gramscian analysis is its concern with the 'commanding heights' of the world, through analysis of the power elite or TMC. Some things matter more than others in the Gramscian account of global governance. This offers a narrative that makes sense of great institutions and suggests they have a logic and purpose which they otherwise may seem to lack.

More broadly, the concern with social forces, as opposed to institutions or organizations in isolation, reinforces the concrete quality of this perspective on global governance. In a simple sense, the Hegemonists are asserting that people, however organized, make global governance, and that we need to appreciate their likely impact. This gives this idea of global governance an immediacy and power others lack.

Underpinning this concern with social forces is the focus on exploitation and inequalities. The commitment to ending deprivation and domination this implies is surely compelling. This highlights just how political the Hegemonist approach to global governance really is, and how far removed from simple assertions of a desire for a better world.

Although gritty and focused on entrenched privilege, the Hegemonists are also able to offer an attractive historical and political-economy analysis of the problems of capitalism which give their approach an optimism and confidence not often found in what are frequently very tentative conceptions of global governance.

A final strength is the comprehensiveness of the conception of global governance, incorporating a range of actors and levels. The central place of ideas, hegemony and blocs of social forces means that global governance is understood as consensual as well as coercive, elite as well as a mass phenomenon.

Weaknesses

There is no getting away from the reality that the origins of this approach to global governance in Marxist thought are not an asset. Although the state socialist regimes of Eastern Europe and the Soviet Union had little to do with Marxist theory, they are not good advertisements for this way of thinking. Before 1989 most educated persons were familiar with Marxist thinking, but that is no longer true since the fall of these regimes. Given this deficit, it is harder to persuade an audience that Hegemonism has a viable and attractive concept of global governance (or anything else).

Does Hegemonism offer a reasoned conception of global power? Is the Gramscian analysis of global governance, especially in its more power elite dimensions, vulnerable to the criticism that it advocates a conspiratorial view of the world, with all things controlled by some omniscient free-masonry of capitalist enforcers? A conspiratorial tone is perhaps most evident in the absence of good supporting empirical research.

In placing emphasis on capitalism, it may be that too little attention is paid to other issues, including the internal dynamics of institutions themselves. In other words, the master narrative may overpower less dramatic but vital dynamics which reflect other social mechanisms and developments.

Conversely, by introducing great emphasis on historical variation and the role of ideas, it may be the case that the Gramscian conception of global governance actually loses focus on core Marxist ideas about how the world works, and is confusing and unclear. As Hegemonism does not offer explicit deductive theories of knowledge, governance and institutions, the audience might be left wondering what exactly it is that is novel about this approach. It seems that Cox and his followers are content to 'bolt on' theories from other schools of thought. But this is not obviously a strong and convincing approach.

Likely future development

The conceptual links between social constructivism and the Gramscian school provide a means for a dialogue on how institutions of global governance are created and decline. The synthesis between these approaches may founder, however, on the Gramscian commitment to a social science Realist notion of capitalism as a social mechanism with its own laws of motion, akin to the laws of the natural universe.

The obvious areas in which Hegemonism and constructivism can come together are in the role of ideas, where both the Gramscians and the constructivists are keenly concerned with the impact of collective ideas. Hegemonism was to a great extent a reaction against an almost exclusive emphasis on structure in Marxist thought during the 1960s and 1970s. Cox, and other Marxist-inspired scholars, suggested ideas matter in a number of ways: that institutions are not independent of our collective ideas about them. Constructivism put emphasis on specific ideas following on from the Liberal debate about the role of ideas as an intervening or residual variable, and, more interestingly, on the role of ideas as the basis for institutions. John Searle systematized this thinking in his conception of social facts (Searle 2005). The legitimacy of the state, a fad, a fashion or the bank run – these are all social facts that, ephemeral as they may seem, are potentially highly consequential, as the global financial crisis that started in 2007 illustrates.

An activist and unilateral American foreign and security policy have created their own opposition, within which a Gramscian worldview can thrive. If American policy becomes more reticent, then a more accommodating perspective on global governance might make more sense to more people. Similar things can be said for the effects of the global financial crisis that started in 2007. This has radicalized some, and it may be that Marxist-inspired thinking is making something of a comeback.

The prospects for Hegemonism are very much dependent on the flexibility of the approach in adapting to other core concerns, such as environmental degradation, which do not sit easily with a modernist worldview in which nature is understood as subject to the determinations of humankind. These ideas might be stitched into a more holistic master narrative which, while avoiding conspiracy, does offer to make sense of a range of discrete challenges within a broader theme such as domination or exploitation.

Overall comments

No theory of global governance can reasonably ignore the existence of capitalism and the driving force this represents on our planet. Hegemonism, whatever its faults, does offer a powerful analysis of global governance premised on the existence of this massive, relentless social system. That it simply points to this system is the greatest asset of Hegemonism. The fact that this reading of Marxist theory is more flexible and historically focused than most Marxist accounts is also important. The flexibility this approach offers and the willingness to think about the dynamics of ideas and institutions, as well as material capabilities, is characteristic.

Because of its origins in Marxism, Hegemonism will always be regarded with scepticism by some observers for whom Marxist thinking died with the Soviet Union. These commentators are right to see the death of that sort of rigid and inflexible model of material determination as a good thing. As an approach to thinking about how society works, structural Marxism was hampered by too much emphasis on structure and too little on human agency. This led to some of the most awkward and implausible writing in western scholarship and to a very poor sense of how politics actually works. What is enormously attractive about the work of Hegemonists is this keen sense for the workings of politics. What the approach does is take the political economy of Marx as developed in *Capital* and link it to his more historical writings, in which this political sense was most acutely developed.

As an approach to global governance, Hegemonism is counter-intuitive. Rather than seeing global governance as a source of improvement and a way out of the problems created by a world of sovereign states, the Gramscian view says that global governance is another enforcement system in a world dominated by capitalism. However, in its focus on change and the tendency for systems to generate their own destruction, the Gramscian account of global governance offers the potential for a transformative view that goes beyond that suggested as feasible by other conceptions analysed in this book.

Scenarios

Our two families have travelled a long way in their attitudes to global governance. In the following hypothetical vignettes, they have adopted a perspective derived from Hegemonism.

Global financial crisis Henry and Sofia wondered whether this was the end of capitalism their parents had always talked about. The Mason children had grown up in a household that bore little resemblance to that of their school friends. Their parents were not interested in the things that concerned most adults. Rather than shiny new cars and expensive vacations the Masons went to political meetings and devoted time to labour organizing. John paid good wages to his vineyard workers and made sure they were not overworked. Sometimes the kids felt a little embarrassed by their parents, but much of the time they were proud of their determination to help the underdog. John and Helen met in college at the University of Massachusetts-Amherst where she studied political science and he took a degree in botany. Both of them were strong critics of the prevailing order and very active politically. John couldn't help but feel happy about the crisis. He had been horrified by the excesses of the housing bubble in the years before the crisis and by the veneration of great wealth that had become such a major part of American culture. He and Helen responded to the crisis by protesting against the volatility of the financial markets outside their local suburban Morgan Stanley branch, accosting the occasional wealthy local residents. On a Friday a few months into the crisis, they took the Long Island Railroad into Penn Station in Manhattan to protest on Wall Street. John and Helen were active bloggers and documented their activities at length. They followed what other people were writing about the crisis and were astonished by the fact that governing elites were as flummoxed by the crisis as everyone else. Given this, the crisis represented a golden opportunity to get their message across.

This was what he had been worried about for years, thought Agastya. The western financial markets are volatile and hostile to family, community and business. Surely the crisis proves this to everyone beyond a shadow of a doubt. Mr Patel, although a businessman, had always been hostile to western corporate capitalism. He had flirted with socialism as a youth. These days he supported Bangalore-based NGOs that shared his views, lobbied against big business at every opportunity and worried about the influence of international capitalism creeping into India through the liberalization process that had started in 1991. Some days he thought the pre-1991 regime might have been better. Agastya was something of a reader and the financial crisis pushed him to re-read Lenin, Hobson and other writers who analysed western imperialism in the early years of the twentieth century. Bhadraa was more radical than her husband. She came from a family steeped in the left politics of India. Identifying injustice and campaigning against it was part of her experience, even as a young girl. She was taught as a child that she had a responsibility to help those who were oppressed. This worldview she passed on to her own children. Although school was quite formal and the children studied long and hard, Aditi in particular had a very well-developed social conscience and it was obvious she was going to grow up like her mother. Vinod, although thinking about cricket during much of his spare time, had excellent general knowledge and was sensitive to how the world was organized. As the crisis developed, Agastya began to see the opportunity it represented to show people that a western-finance-dominated world was not inevitable and that alternative ways of organizing government, business and the community were desirable and necessary to avoid the depth of problems in Europe and America.

Climate change   The Masons had been persuaded that climate change was a reality. John thought he could detect it in his vineyards if he looked at records going back to the late

1960s. But the Masons were not environmentalists. For them, global warming was a symptom of a destructive global capitalist system that was just as happy to use and abuse the environment as it was to do this to people. So, although the planet was under threat, it wasn't humans that were doing this. It was instead a very specific system that dominated people and the planet that gave rise to this destruction. But to John and Helen climate change represented a good opportunity, like the financial crisis, to get the message out that it was the system lying behind these problems that had to be tackled. Their blog focused on corporate pollution and carbon generation, rather than the problems in domestic houses and consumption. John was happy to travel for hours to get the evidence he needed and he was equally willing to give presentations on the issue whenever an opportunity arose. Henry found this approach to global warming more convincing than the usual line. He was eager to pursue this as far as he could and became involved in the World Social Forum, the great rival to the World Economic Forum that meets in Davos, Switzerland, each January. He made plans to attend the event in order to make his case about climate change. His sister Sofia was most concerned about the impact of climate change on marginal workers, especially the sort of people who picked grapes during harvest at her father's vineyard. Global warming was making the harvest less reliable and making the income these workers received less secure.

The Patels were angry about the impact of corporate capitalism on the world's climate. They were astonished by the amount of pollution produced by just a few countries. The US in particular produced carbon out of all proportion to its population. Agastya thought that global solutions would be needed to bring this to an end. The United States had, however, proven remarkably resistant to global standards in this area. But, given the global nature of the problem, there must be a global response. Failing this, Mr Patel continued to push his view that small business was different from big business and not likely to produce global problems. Bhadraa was more activated by the issue. She was aware of the effect of climate change on rural life. The greater incidence of

natural disaster, drought and flood were creating a new wave
of urbanization in India, driven by the unreliability of rural
sustenance. Like children almost everywhere, the Patel off-
spring were concerned about how the weather was changing
and the long-run impact of pumping carbon into the atmo-
sphere. For them, it certainly brought home the importance
of politics. But, unlike their friends who did not make the
connections, they saw the issue very much in terms of a global
order that placed a value on some things and had been happy
to neglect carbon emissions. Aditi and Vinod took a more
social or structural view than most of their peer group. They
were critical consumers of mass media, and were increasingly
vocal about the unreflective adoration shown in commercial
media for consumption and waste. They tried to convert their
friends to the view that much of what passed for entertain-
ment directed at them was often little more than skilful
product placement designed to get them to buy more and
more goods they did not need.

Development   The Masons were very conscious of the
way international trade and finance were organized. In their
view, the way things were ordered reproduced a system in
which some countries received most benefits while many
others remained poor and disenfranchised. There was nothing
natural about this, thought Helen. The children were enthusiasts for fair trade at school. The focus for John was the
international financial institutions, the IMF and World Bank.
Rather than being agents of improvement in the lives of
people in the developing world, John saw these organizations
as transmitting and enforcing a particular approach to economic life which was intolerant of alternatives like subsis-
tence farming. In his view, the lending of these agencies
encouraged a cash-crop economy based on exporting. This
made farmers in these countries reliant on markets in far-
away rich countries, often neglecting the production of basic
foodstuffs for their local community. The results of these
policies, as John saw it, were food shortages, famine and
migration. Being involved in the global economy could,
rather than foster development, destroy poor countries,
reducing their ability to feed and house their own populations. In John's view, the least that should be done was a

wholesale restructuring of these institutions. They needed both to be accountable to borrowers, as the Cosmopolitans want, and to change policy toward a more sustainable vision of economic life in which producing cash crops for export was no longer understood as the gold standard. John could recall reading about the New International Economic Order debate in the 1970s, in which former colonies sought a rebalancing in things like commodity prices so as to transfer more wealth to their hands. For both John and Helen, this sort of rebalancing was needed still, together with a systematic understanding of the causes of the imbalances in the first place.

Development was a topic that was close to home for many Indians, including the Patels. The family were very much aware of the hard road India had taken to economic growth and had views on the global order that, in their view, had acted as a barrier to this process for so long, keeping Indians and citizens of other developing countries poor. Amongst Agastya's older friends, it was common to think of this issue in conspiratorial terms – rich countries colluded to keep rich by exploiting the poor. Certainly Agastya and Bhadraa were willing to go along with this simple idea. But there was more to the story than this. For them, capitalism was at the heart of the story. Although it was organized with a core and a periphery, there was pain and suffering at the core too. The problem was the nature of the system itself and that is what they wanted to change. For them, it was not enough that India was shining. It was important that the system that had kept India down for so long be dismantled. Mr Patel promoted these ideas in the neighbourhood club he visited, although it seemed to him that most people were more interested in getting rich themselves rather than changing the system. Perhaps the most radical member of the family when it came to development was eldest daughter Aditi. She found what her father had to say applied well in her history and geography classes, but was very much contradicted in economics. When she asked her teachers about development, she found they mostly repeated the idea that market solutions were best. Given the financial crisis, she no longer shared this easy faith. Increasingly, Aditi focused on the World Social Forum as a venue for her concerns and she grew determined to participate in the annual meeting of the WSF in Brazil.

Security John never bought into the idea that the Iraq invasion was about oil, but he certainly was not convinced by the Weapons of Mass Destruction claim, a view which events subsequently supported. His own take on the invasion was that the military wanted it, especially the US Air Force, because it would give them back their operational flexibility after more than a decade of monitoring the no-fly zones in northern and southern Iraq. He could just see senior military officers pushing for this option. In any case, John was not a great supporter of his country's military. He had avoided ROTC in college and was horrified by the frequent wars the US had engaged in during the years since Vietnam. He saw the US military very much as a global enforcement agency for a particular type of capitalist order with the US as hegemon. Although utterly horrified by the 9/11 attacks, he saw these not as irrational acts but as the worst imaginable resistance to a US-dominated global capitalist order. Rather than crushing the terrorists, he wanted, like a lot of the US academic establishment, to try and understand the motivations behind these terrible acts. This more structural view of security was at the heart of his thinking about most phenomena. Helen was interested in security too and had often argued that the US would do best to imitate Sweden's defensive posture, which eschewed offensive weapons for those with a purely defensive use. This would preclude regime change and expeditionary forces but that made good sense to her. More pragmatically, John and Helen highlighted spending on military procurement in the US and the waste and failure this often seemed to produce. Their blogs on military procurement were very popular and people were increasingly citing their research in online fora on military policy.

The Patels, like most of their friends of all sorts of political inclinations, supported India's long tradition of non-alignment. They were saddened by communal conflict, terrorism and border tensions with Pakistan. Like the Masons, the Patels were never a military family. But in India the military was a bit different. It was bound up with the creation and existence of the state in ways familiar in other developing countries. However, the Indians had been very sensible about equipment and had avoided spending too much on high-tech weaponry. Nuclear weapons were the exception to this rule, but their possession again seems to the Patels to be as much about nation-building in India as about security. Agastya and Bhadraa had strongly opposed the invasions of Afghanistan and Iraq. In their view, these actions were bound to produce the mayhem and loss of life that followed. Greater introspection following 9/11 would have produced a better outcome than the march to war. They had both protested against war in the streets of Bangalore and even went to Delhi to protest outside the US embassy. The Patels thought old-fashioned power balancing might give rise to a more peaceful world. The rise of China in particular – although, in some parts of the Indian elite, perceived as a threat – might serve to modify US behaviour and reduce the tendency of the US to engage in unilateral actions. Although a new Cold War was most unappealing, this had to be set against the costs of having just one superpower. Agastya did observe that a problem with power balancing, as had existed, for example, during the nineteenth century in Europe, was that it tended to lead to arms races. Although the Concert of Europe had been effective for a very long time, it was followed by one of the worst wars in history.

Gender relations Helen Mason had considered herself a Feminist since she was seventeen. It just seemed like commonsense to her, although coming from a family of strong women might have been an important influence. She did a women's studies class in college but this had only given her some ideas to organize her thoughts better. When she met John his ideas about capitalism were new to her and they forced her to think about the relationship between gender and capitalism. In time she decided that traditional gender relations cheapened the costs of living for capitalism, and thus capitalism had an interest in perpetuating sexism and the exploitation of women. If you were going to obtain women's liberation, you were going to have to break this link with capitalism. Initially, John found his new girlfriend's ideas about women's rights an irritating distraction. Surely, he reasoned, the real issue was the effects of capitalism. Women's rights were at best a side issue. But Helen was patient with him. He read some of her books and attended a talk or two and eventually he became a convert to the idea that gender relations and capitalism were closely linked. This intellectual consensus between the two of them became a key part of their mutual understanding and trust. It underpinned how they brought up their children and their approach to other people. For John, incorporating gender relations had brought his big talk about capitalism down to earth in a useful way. For Helen, thinking about capitalism gave her concerns with gender more history and geographical specificity. For both of them, gender really provided a good angle for criticizing the system when a full attack on capitalism would not have been given a hearing.

Agastya's home life was different from that of his friends. Their wives cooked and cleaned for them. Agastya had not had a 'normal' life for years. His wife was a local leader of a women's rights organization, and very active. She was often not there to do the sort of domestic work that Indian women normally did in the household. This had been hard to adapt to for Agastya, but he had come to support his wife's work very strongly. It was hard for Agastya to be both a critic of global exploitation and a perpetrator of it on the domestic level. Bhadraa's current focus was on securing adequate public washing and laundering facilities in Bangalore for the city's poor and indigent. She had worked hard to have the current disintegrating public ablutions rebuilt bigger and better. Although a very basic function, you have to start with such things, thought Bhadraa. Her next task was to improve electricity generation, which was still very fragile. She was starting to have some impact on city politicians, who were learning that this modest woman was well informed and determined to make improvements. They had started to rely on her good judgement and excellent research. There was even talk that Bhadraa should consider running for office herself. Because of their mother and her activities, the children were aware of gender issues from an early age. Their father encouraged them in this but also challenged them to think about gender in wider, global terms and to seek the sources of power and politics on this level as much as on the local one. The children, especially the twins, often found themselves instructing others about the issue of gender relations and how this form of oppression could not be detached from other forms of exploitation.

Problems to consider

In examining Hegemonism and global governance, you might want to discuss the following. First, Hegemonism is built on the conceptual foundations provided by Marx, Gramsci and other sympathetic authors. In what ways does an analysis of global governance with origins in the Marxist analysis of capitalism offer fresh new insights into the mechanisms of global order? Second, does the focus on social forces in the first instance, as opposed to organizations, bring something to the analysis of global governance, or is this a distraction from the real substance of global authority? Last, what do the Hegemonists actually say about the mechanisms of global governance more specifically? Is their major contribution in terms of the debate about ideas, or do you consider this approach to offer little or any benefit to understanding and enhancing global governance?

Further reading

You could read the classic works of Marx and Gramsci. But an interesting route into this way of thinking, which might be more accessible, is Robert W. Cox's *Production, Power, and World Order* (1987), or Cox's essays collected in *Approaches to World Order* (with Sinclair 1996). In a similar vein, you might also read Stephen Gill's *Power and Resistance in the New World Order* (2008). However, the most exciting work about global governance written by one of the Gramscians is almost certainly that by Craig N. Murphy. Murphy's work is exceptional because it mixes an exhaustive understanding of the institutions and history of global governance with an equally exhaustive knowledge of the institutions of capitalism. Three works that will excite you are Murphy, *International Organization and Industrial Change: Global Governance since 1850* (1994), Murphy, 'Global Governance: Poorly Done and Poorly Understood' (2000), and Murphy, *Global Institutions, Marginalization, and Development* (2005). The 1994 volume is a true *tour de force* on the subject.

7
Feminism

Feminism offers a very different and exciting way to understand global governance. Although it is only just starting to emerge, this view of what global governance is and what it might become has much to offer both as a critique of mainstream views and as a positive statement of what global governance could be. Unlike most other ways of thinking about global governance, Feminists' views begin with the most basic ideas about human identity. From these ideas they generate criticisms of how the world is organized based on the inequities they find in these basic relationships. The Feminist view of global governance is thus one that starts at the ground level with people and then analytically moves upward to consider the broader dynamics of how the world is organized, based on this understanding of social relationships.

The great challenge with Feminism is that it is so very different from mainstream thinking like Institutionalism. While being rooted in human relationships gives the approach great strengths and makes it very attractive to adherents – much like Hegemonism – the way of thinking about global governance is very different and may seem marginal or irrelevant to some. In this chapter I want to show you that Feminism offers a thoughtful and potentially powerful way of thinking about global governance which offers to shed new light on how our world is organized. This way of thinking, we should concede, is greatly outnumbered in terms of adherents by mainstream thought, but that does not mean we cannot find in it valuable things to say about global governance.

Background

The Feminist perspective on global governance is built upon a rich tradition of thought and action, starting with Mary Wollstonecraft in the second half of the eighteenth century. In the 1960s and 1970s there was a surge of political writing by Feminists advocating change, including work by Shulamith Firestone, Betty Friedan, Sheila Rowbotham and Germaine Greer, amongst others. This was a period of great social change in the developed world as prosperity encouraged the pursuit of civil, social and political rights by a greater segment of the population. Activism by women in pursuit of equal pay, the legal right to own property and control of reproduction followed an earlier period of agitation in pursuit of the right to vote during the first few decades of the twentieth century.

More recently, this tradition of thought, often philosophically and methodologically sophisticated, provided the foundation for the development of Feminist thinking in sociology and political science, especially in the field of international relations and the sub-field of international political economy, by authors such as J. Ann Tickner, V. Spike Peterson, Sandra Whitworth, Diane Elson, Isabella Bakker and Jacqui True. These scholars undertake academic work with analytical and normative objectives. But Feminism is by no means only an intellectual activity in a university setting. This vibrant intellectual activism has been matched by significant political activism, especially in the developing world, crystallizing around the UN conferences on women, especially the Beijing meeting of 1995, and the Millennium Development Goals all UN member states agreed to meet by 2015.

Purpose

As we have seen, most thinking about global governance is undertaken from a problem-solving point of view. That is, the vast bulk of writing about global governance has quite limited objectives – to make the world we live in a little better, to make it function more effectively, to update things that seem no longer relevant or useful. Feminism also wants to make the world we live in better. Feminism, considered as a worldview, as a political project, and as a scholarly position, certainly does not reject improvement of the world we live in. This differentiates Feminism from Hegemonism, which has always offered a trenchant critique of attempts to reform the existing system in its ambition for a new system.

What do Feminists want to change? The core concern in the Feminism worldview is the idea that women in both the developed and developing world suffer overt and covert discrimination and exploitation by men. This problem pervades human institutions and seems to cross epochs of human history. But rather than see this as a natural condition, Feminism wants to transform this situation and eliminate the problem. This takes both problem-solving forms such as the Millennium Development Goals and more radical, critical forms, involving a transformation of society away from dominant patriarchal forms. Feminist perspectives vary in terms of their purpose along this range. In the context of global governance, Feminism typically seeks to change institutions and processes to recognize the problems they have made for women. In this sense, much of the agenda for change is in keeping with Schechter's policy-relevant critical theory I talked about earlier.

Puzzles

Three puzzles dominate Feminism's work on global governance, for both activists and academics. The first is establishing links between the public and private, the wider world and the home, which mainstream analyses deny. This is the meat and potatoes of all Feminist analyses of international relations. It is very challenging because global governance is defined by the mainstream as not private, and as having no intimate connotations. Feminist scholars and activists think mainstream analysis has ignored the issue of gender and how institutions like the IMF reproduce the domination of women.

The second puzzle is trying to understand how gender, which is the common concern of Feminism, permeates institutions of global governance. Unlike, say, Institutionalism, which does not impute a logic to global governance, Feminism identifies gender, and the domination of women, as a core feature of global governance. The problem is, how does this actually work and with what implications for women? Given how the understanding of what global governance is, and how it works, is so dominated by technocratic views, this puzzle is challenging.

This rather timeless concern to show that institutions are biased against women is matched by a third puzzle, which seeks an analysis of globalization, or the post-Bretton Woods era, and how this has changed global governance, accelerating processes of gender exploitation and vulnerability via, especially, the major international economic agencies, such as the IMF, World Bank and WTO. This concern with restructuring and the current direction of policy gives the Feminist view of global governance added poignancy.

Level of analysis and actors

In principle, Feminism's level of analysis is really quite intimate. Rather than focusing on broad historical structures, Feminism focuses on the gender divide and how the institutions and processes of global governance reflect this engendering, in which women typically come off second-best. Of course, when this phenomenon is generalized across the globe, as Feminism says is the case, it no longer seems quite so intimate. For the most part Feminist analysis and activism focus on very similar institutions of concern to other perspectives. Like Hegemonism, there is a strong awareness of the centrality of work, the labour process and economic life.

For many Feminist analysts and activists, links are drawn between capitalism and patriarchy, or the system of gender oppression of women. The idea here is that patriarchy, or the structure of male privilege, supports and is supported by the capitalist mode of production. Female work to reproduce the household through childcare, cooking and cleaning supports the production system, and has historically enabled men to operate in the public world of paid work while women have been confined to the home. Today, when both men and women work for wages, women still assume an unequal share of the domestic, unpaid work.

Unlike most approaches to global governance, Feminism focuses on the public sphere and the private sphere in the same analysis. This is interesting because for most ways of thinking about global governance the private sphere is, by definition, not part of the equation. For Feminism, we can only understand the public in its relationship with the private, even though the private sphere of reproduction is typically defined as private and therefore not political. Feminism wants to tell us that the relationships in the private sphere are unequal, exploitative and therefore highly political. It is the task of Feminism to highlight these.

For Feminists of most persuasions, the state remains a central actor in global governance despite post-Bretton Woods globalization. It has a major role in managing the public–private link. As for many other perspectives on global governance, the state remains a key support for globalization and a stepping stone to intrastate forms of power. For activists, the state is central to trying to make change as it is the one institution in society which is able to redefine what is deemed political. This is a vital capacity and one most ways of thinking about global governance are concerned to highlight.

As with the state, Feminist thinkers about global governance see international institutions and regimes as crucial. These are the places in which global governance is engendered. These places must therefore be closely analysed by Feminists to understand how this works in different contexts and to develop strategies for countering engendering, such as gender mainstreaming, which takes into account the potential impact of policy change on men and women. For all their history of faults, institutions are vital as places in which how things are done can be contested. This makes institutions important places in which the struggle for change can take place.

Assumptions

Like the Hegemonists considered in chapter 6, Feminist thinking about global governance seems to assume the existence of pervasive social mechanisms like patriarchy and capitalism underpinning human relations. Structuralism like this is common in international relations. Realism, to cite the classic example, assumes the existence of anarchy. Anarchy produces imperatives for all states, regardless of other factors, suggests Realism. But the inclination to impute structure or function in Feminism is tempered by an appreciation, also commonly found in Hegemonism, for the different historical forms assumed by social relations. Just as capitalism may take different forms in different places and times, so too can patriarchy and the engendering of social relations be different in different places and times.

Feminist approaches to global governance do not assume, as might be thought, that eliminating gender domination will produce utopia. In other words, Feminist thinking about global governance does not ignore or neglect other potentially vital issues in global governance, such as bureaucratic politics. Gender is not the only issue in global governance. It is just that gender is, like other private or personal dimensions, marginalized by these other approaches, and so it is the job of Feminism to correct this problem.

Feminism does not accept the idea that international institutions are typically neutral politically. Instead, Feminism assumes the pervasiveness of politics in global governance. Based on insights from its acute awareness of gender issues, Feminism, in both scholarly and activist forms, is critical of technocratic talk about international institutions, instead seeing hidden political dynamics.

Ontology

Gender is at the centre of the Feminist account of what matters when thinking about global governance. Gender is different from sex. As things stand, sex – whether you are male or female – is biologically determined. In the absence of medical intervention, this determines whether you can bear children or not. But gender in the Feminist view is a social construct and is not biological. As a social construct, gender reflects a political struggle between men and women over who determines what work is done and by whom. Child rearing as opposed to bearing is not determined by biology but by social roles. That women also take most responsibility for rearing, as well as bearing, children is a result of being given this role, not a result of nature's dictates.

At the other end of the spectrum in terms of intuitiveness, participation of women is also a key thing that matters in the Feminist conception of global governance. While certainly not sufficient in itself to bring the sort of change most Feminists seek, it is necessary that women are present in global governance institutions and processes for there to be reform.

Although primarily interested in gender and how institutions and processes disempower women, the concern of Feminism with the characteristics of people and the social construction of their political circumstances makes the approach open to investigating links with race and class. In this sense, the ontology of Feminism is open to development. For this reason we can easily draw links with Hegemonism, but also with Post-colonial theory.

Post-colonial theory is also built on identifying a social construct (Hobson 2007). In this case the construct is of non-western people as backward and incompetent because they do not accept Enlightenment assumptions as progressive and universally acceptable, but see them as parochial. Think of attitudes to the place of religion in society, or the view taken by many Islamic scholars of interest-earning banking systems, for example. Post-colonialism sums up this view in its concept of Eurocentrism. Eurocentrism has a similar status in Post-colonial thinking to gender in Feminism. It is seen as pervasive and typically unconscious by adherents. It is a structure that pervades the global order, serving to reproduce it. Like Feminism, about which Post-colonial thought is at times highly critical for its own Eurocentric assumptions, the objective for Post-colonial thought is a recognition of this problem and an emphasis by scholars on the issues of identity and culture, something oddly lacking in Hegemonism.

Implications

As with Hegemonism, for Feminism the discussion of global governance does not start with the view that the existing reality of global governance is necessarily positive or liberating. Like other institutions, global governance, be it the World Bank, the World Health Organization or the Law of the Sea, is inscribed with gender. Feminism approaches these institutions aware of this latent politics. For activists and academics alike, challenging the engendering of global governance is vital. For many Feminists, global governance institutions provide a place, like state institutions, in which they can make their case that institutions are engendered. In this sense, although structured to serve gender domination from the outset, global governance institutions do provide the opportunity for contesting that oppression.

As we have seen, much of the debate about global governance in the mainstream takes place at an elevated level, through discussions of broad policy. This is the common-sense assumption about global governance: that it is elite politics. But Feminism rejects this view as mistaken. An intriguing implication of global governance as conceived in Feminism is that it redirects our attention away from the macro or elite level to the micro level of the person and their identity, although collectively conceived rather than in terms of individual personality. This is an interesting implication of Feminism – it opens up an entirely new level or field of enquiry for the observer. By refocusing global governance in this way, Feminism suggests we think about global governance as a much more pervasive phenomenon than we did before. International institutions, regimes and NGOs now fit into a much more political map of politics than they did before thinking in terms of the Feminist conception of global governance.

Applications

Feminism has become a ubiquitous way of thinking in the humanities and social sciences over the past few decades. No longer are scholars with this perspective excluded, although the degree of their acceptance varies. Being trained in a well-recognized discipline seems to be important, with scholars in women's studies or gender studies seemingly finding less support for what they do than other academics. International relations in particular has experienced growth in Feminist thought. The second wave of this work, since around 1990, has pursued a more specific empirical research and conceptual agenda and has started to address the problem of global governance. In the policy world too, activists for women's equality have made much progress in getting their agenda accepted at all levels of government in the developed world, and in international institutions.

In recent years women's interests and representation have been promoted via gender mainstreaming (Hoskyns 2008). This follows a succession of earlier efforts to empower women, such as equal treatment in employment and positive action to compensate particular groups of disadvantaged women. Gender mainstreaming is not a specific policy measure. Think of it instead as a question that is mandated in policy-making, research and development, and implementation in institutions like the United Nations system. In this way it serves much like, or is supposed to work like, the financial controls that institutions have. UN Women (the 'United Nations Entity for Gender Equality and the Empowerment of Women') sees gender mainstreaming as 'ensuring that gender perspectives and attention to the goal of gender equality are central to all activities . . .' (UN Women 2012).

Differences of emphasis within Feminism

As Rai and Waylen note, Feminism has many different tendencies, many 'different feminisms' such as Liberal, socialist, radical, Post-colonial, black and lesbian (Rai and Waylen 2008b: 3). But as an approach to global governance, Feminism remains novel. The Feminist global governance literature, such as it is, is better characterized by what it has in common rather than great cleavages between divergent schools of thought. What unites this way of thinking about global governance, of course, is the commitment to gender as the core Feminist insight. Gender still very much serves as the intellectual touchstone of this emerging way of thinking about global governance. But for some Feminists, especially Liberals, participation in institutions, rather than structural reform or a direct challenge to the system, is their focus. Others are very much concerned with combining their analysis with that of the political economy of capitalism. This work is as much about the crisis of capitalism and the efforts to restructure production as it is narrowly about gender.

Strengths

What do we make of Feminism as an understanding of global governance? It has a number of strengths. One is the links it draws between the very low and concrete level of the person and broader structural claims about global processes. Everyone can relate to some of the stories Feminism tells about gender politics. Making the personal political gives an immediacy and power to the claims of activists and academics that makes their broader claims seem much more measured than some other perspectives. We view elite institutions with a more critical eye given this account.

Perhaps the most important strength is to offer in gender a 'master concept' which gives power to the claims of this perspective. Gender is not a simple idea or easy to grasp but once it has been accepted by the audience it cuts through a great deal, much like the Realist concept of anarchy in international relations. Activists and scholars of global governance can mine this concept for a lot of political and analytical purchase on global governance, as Marxists do with exploitation.

Typical of Feminism is sensitivity to actual circumstances and links between gender oppression and other forms of political exclusion. Feminism has a concrete and empirical quality which makes it fit well with historical analyses. Starting with the personal provides great discipline on conceptual claims, making them more relevant than they would otherwise be. Feminism does not usually claim to be the only form of oppression, and thus fits well with other accounts.

Weaknesses

Feminism has problems too. An unsympathetic critic might suggest the focus on gender and engendering of global governance institutions is somewhat monotonous. As the 'master concept', it is subject to lengthy discussion and this might seem to be to the exclusion of other issues and problems. The weakness is probably derived from the necessity for Feminism to make its case against opposition and indifference.

To some it might seem that the links between global governance and gender are somewhat tenuous. Nobody would deny that they exist – but exactly how important are they relative to other issues and problems? This problem may reflect a relative paucity of good empirical research so far in the first generation of Feminist research on global governance. We can expect this issue to diminish as more good social science is published by global governance scholars influenced by Feminism.

Perhaps the most challenging weakness relates to the concept of gender itself. This 'master concept' of Feminism seems to pervade everything. Exactly how this occurs often seems to be unclear. In other words, it always just seems to be there, somewhat akin to Marx's notion of exploitation. For the sceptic, the question is how this occurs and whether gender is more of an issue in some places and at some times than others. This weakness is a challenge for all approaches that posit a structural condition, and can be addressed through further empirical research which is designed to show the origins and mechanisms of transmission of gender, and how gender works to produce oppression.

Likely future development

Where will the gendered view of global governance go in future? It is certainly likely to retain and enhance its popularity amongst activists as a more mutual, communal and potentially multilateral approach to global governance than most of its competitors. The approach is not an elite project and so it has appeal to those who are critics of elite control of politics. This is a vital element for Feminism and one to be preserved.

A key step in expanding this appeal is reaching out to Post-colonial scholars in the developing world. This will make the analysis better and help to avoid the criticism that Feminist approaches to global governance are purely a western debate and ignore the many forms of oppression for those in the developing world.

Much more good empirical work is necessary. At present the approach is in the early stages of development and not a lot of good research has been completed. Completing and publishing this work will give the approach greater scholarly credibility and standing as a research programme. This comment would be the same for any research tradition in its early stages.

A vital element of this research programme is the development of a series of tractable mid-range concepts to fit with gender. Gender is a very broad account and needs to be supported with lesser mechanisms and concepts that are well founded and persuasive. Much of this will emerge from finding out how it is that gender becomes cemented into global governance (and other institutions).

Overall comments

Feminism is a thoughtful and perceptive approach to thinking about global governance. It starts from the personal experience of at least half the human population. It links the concrete experience of people with the broad structures of global governance. It offers a 'master concept' in the form of gender, which is useful in penetrating the surface of global governance in search of its substance.

The approach is certainly counter-intuitive and offers a more analytical view of global governance than many approaches, which tend to start from the intuitively obvious and then generalize. The seriousness of the approach does make it hard to follow the connections drawn at times and it is easy to imagine the non-sympathetic reader would dismiss Feminism as far-fetched. This would be an unfortunate error.

We should acknowledge that Feminist activists are well entrenched in global governance institutions. Most of the major institutions have acknowledged and accepted their criticisms at least to some extent. Whether this means real influence for the activists or mere lip service is an open question.

To achieve its potential in the academic world, much more good research needs to be done by Feminism-influenced scholars. The work done so far has been very valuable in establishing the foundation for the work to come (Whitworth 1994). This needs to show how gender is relevant, and develop mid-range concepts which support gender and provide further support for a research programme. Certainly some of this is already published, but a much stronger body of literature is needed.

Scenarios

Our two families have found themselves thinking in new and surprising ways as they have adopted different perspectives on global governance. In the following, Feminism is the core worldview from which these vignettes are derived.

Global financial crisis The adult Patels were astonished by the global financial crisis. Like a lot of other people they had 'drunk the Kool-Aid' and were uncritical supporters of globalization and the prosperity they associated with it. Look what it had done for them, they thought. The effects of the crash were such that the Patels went through something of a crisis of self-confidence and questioned a lot of the things they did and the people and institutions they admired. Agastya and Bhadraa contrasted the world of high finance with the world of micro-finance small lending they knew from the villages. Micro-finance was not a perfect world by any means, but they much preferred it to the world of macro-finance. What they liked about it – especially Bhadraa – was that ordinary women were at the centre of it.

The global financial crisis made the Patels wonder about the gendering of institutions, in the sense that much of global finance seemed hostile to community, something so central to their lives. It made them wonder whether greater involvement by women in many of the governing institutions of our world might not be a bad thing. The family were able to think back to their rural origins. Yes, there was plenty of unhappiness there. That is why they moved to the city, after all. But what worked well was the sense that people were taken care of. Agastya and Bhadraa discussed whether care was a missing element in their lives in the city. More broadly, they considered whether this responsibility was missing from national politics and global governance too. They certainly believed in self-help, but discrimination was something they knew well from caste as well as gender sources, so they saw value in collective corrective measures.

The Masons were fairly careful, frugal people. When the global financial crisis unfolded, they too had quite a strong adverse reaction to the culture of Wall Street. John had grown up watching the movie *Wall Street* and had clear memories of Michael Douglas's character Gordon Gekko telling an audience that 'greed is good'. Unlike many of his contemporaries – who, to director Oliver Stone's regret, had idealized Gekko and his views – John saw Wall Street as the problem. Helen's view centred on women's participation, or the lack thereof. Not nearly enough women were in Wall Street. That's why banking kept on producing crises. What was needed were more women like Meredith Whitney, the analyst who is alleged to have called the sub-prime crisis first.

For Henry and Sofia, the global financial crisis had been a formative event. Henry had secretly idealized the men in the expensive suits. The idea of moving from the rural North Fork of Long Island to 'the city' was very exciting to him. But watching homes being foreclosed, unemployment grow and the misery of many families he knew changed him. He picked up on the idea his parents and sister talked about that the lack of female involvement had somehow made Wall Street the problem it was at that moment of bail-outs and financial collapse. This would probably change him forever.

Climate change   The Masons had changed much in recent years. Like most people, they had spent their lives preoccupied by work and the household tasks that filled the time. But, unlike many other families they knew, they watched little TV. They had cancelled their cable TV subscription a few years ago and now only watched TV when they were drawn to something. When Helen started getting interested in Feminism the tone around the house shifted. Things became more active and more political. They started reading more books and visiting serious internet websites. Sofia spent less time on her celebrity webpages, which used to transfix her. As Helen was getting more concerned about the participation and representation of women, John, Henry and Sofia were getting worried about the climate. Part of this was driven by John's dinner-table stories from work, in which he outlined how the changing weather was affecting his vineyards. He was worried about any change in the maritime nature of North Fork's climate. Henry and Sofia were much more aware of climate than earlier generations and were aware how vulnerable they were to change. Long Island is really a vast sand spit, low lying and vulnerable to storms. What was going on in the household was that the family was making a switch from the dominant culture of the short term, of what a social scientist might call a synchronic worldview of quick profits and quick excitement, to a very different mental framework. In this new framework, which they could all trace to Helen's developing interest in Feminism, they started to value longer-term and connected thinking, increasingly thinking in terms of John's world of viticulture. This new thinking, which a social scientist might label diachronic, was leading them to think very differently about the structures and relationships necessary at the global level in order to combat the human-induced climate problems that threatened them.

Diachronic thinking was not far away from the Patels' thoughts either, as they contemplated the impact of climate change on Bangalore and their relatives back home. But for them the issue was more about gender. Bhadraa was in close touch with relatives at home. Tragically, there had been a spate of peasant farmer suicides in her village because of crop failure. These bad harvests were attributed to global warming. The problem was that the tenant farmers had to borrow money from money lenders until the harvest came in. Repeat crop failure put them in such a bad situation that a number of the local farmers known to Bhadraa's family had committed suicide, unable to face their circumstances. The death of these men was a terrible tragedy for everyone they knew. But it also had quite specific effects on the women. Often, in order to pay off the landlords and money lenders, these women were forced into the sex business and into near-servitude. These consequences were not talked about openly, but because Bhadraa was educated into seeing the engendering of things she was able to make the connections. Encouraged by this knowledge, Bhadraa approached local offices of an international NGO with her story, trying to seek their assistance in addressing the disaster.

Development   The Patels thought about their business a lot, and how to get on in life. This they shared with most people they knew. But it was hard to be Indian without thinking about things a little bit more systematically. Part of being Indian is a national story about conquest, foreign domination and national independence. Economic life, during the years of state control prior to 1991, was dominated by large family-run firms. This was still true in India after the state stepped back from protectionism in the early 1990s. The Patels were small-scale operators. They had started their firm from the ground up with few connections and no patronage. It was a tough business cleaning, and highly competitive. Growing in these circumstances had made the family aware of the challenges faced by others. Agastya and Bhadraa were both very critical of the large family combines, seeing them as shutting out small business. Feminism taught Bhadraa to see the domination of the family combines in terms of power. The Patels were worried that the Indian state had put a lot of faith in the combines. What about rural development, what about jobs for the poor, the unskilled, the illiterate? Agastya and Bhadraa thought a very different approach to development, which placed emphasis on the small enterprise and on the work of women, would make more sense for the vast bulk of India's poor, who would probably never have a stake in the urban world connected to the global economy.

The Masons were involved in small-scale intensive agriculture through John's work in viticulture. This gave them a predisposition toward the small scale and toward local forms of development. One day Sofia came home from school talking about development in Africa and how major Chinese firms were buying up resources and precious minerals. The family had a long discussion of development and what it meant. The family decided it meant more than just rising incomes for people, it also meant that people would have more freedom to make choices, to move, to enjoy better health, to get away from oppressive conditions. This was a holistic view of development, one that fitted well with Feminism. The family further discussed how this way of pursuing development could be furthered, given how much emphasis there was on growth pure and simple. The Masons agreed that the best approach would be to start in rural communities, where most people in the developing world lived, and to start with the needs and desires of people there, rather than with the idea that everybody should simply move to the city. Sofia decided to do a project on this for school, not to try and convince her classmates of the moral rightness of the position, but instead to explore how exactly an approach like this could work, in quite concrete terms. In developing her presentation, Sofia acquired a lot of knowledge and some insight into the problem, which she would use in the years ahead to develop her vocational aspirations.

Security   On the face of it security is not a gendered issue, is it? It is a technical and political issue and we should be thinking about high politics when we ponder security issues – right? This common-sense view, which a lot of men she knew repeated, did not wash with Bhadraa. She had read Enloe (2001) and she saw things differently. Nearby was the Indian Air Force's Yelahanka Air Force Station and several other military installations. Around these bases, Bhadraa knew, lived a whole community of sex workers, providing services to military personnel. So, through her eyes, educated as she was in Feminism, high politics and gender were not mutually exclusive. One went with the other. Watching CNN, Bhadraa knew that problems with bases were found all over the world and were just as much an issue with UN peace-keeping troops as they were with national soldiers. Bhadraa had worked with a local NGO that gave health care to the sex workers and she was eager to see a global framework for this through UN Women, but she knew an initiative like this would run up against a lot of opposition.

The Masons were fairly sceptical about the concept of security these days. Helen's developing interest in Feminism had made them all look again at many of their assumptions about the world. Why was so little said in the western media about the hidden victims of war, the women and children killed in drone attacks on Islamic militants in Pakistan and Afghanistan? This interest in the hidden stories of war, especially in relation to women, had driven Helen to pursue further studies at Hunter College in New York City one day a week. This was quite an undertaking for her, involving a long train ride on the Long Island Rail Road and the noise and bustle of the great city. At Hunter she talked to other students and started to develop ideas for doing research of her own into alternative or critical conceptions of security that would allow her to pursue her interests and her belief that women as well as men were involved in security.

At school, Henry and Sofia ran into a few problems because of some of the ideas they had picked up from their mother about security. They did not share the rather uncritical view most of their classmates had about the issue, which seemed to involve sending in the B-52 bombers and US Navy SEAL teams as often as possible. What Henry and Sofia talked about, and which was not well received by a number of their classmates, was the other side of security: the motivations of those on the other side and the issue of 'collateral damage', or the unintended casualties of war. Henry in particular suggested there must be scope for some sort of global regulation of response to security threats, more effective than the UN Security Council. What Henry and Sofia wanted was a more thorough understanding of security and a more comprehensive response to the issue, which took account of the Feminist view of the problem.

Gender relations   Bhadraa Patel had learnt about Feminism from her mother, as a child. The distinction between sex and gender was common-sense to her. It was something that became an organizing principle in her life, although not always with the full support of her husband or wider family. Bhadraa was determined to pursue recognition of gender and the discriminatory realities faced by Indian women. Although she did not have much free time, her work for Transparency International (TI) India was very important to her. In the seven years she had worked for this NGO, she had come face to face with gender discrimination again and again. Often this was in the form of unspoken assumptions that she, as a woman, could not be serious about TI because of her family ties – which was her 'real work', after all.

Aditi was no stranger to gender discrimination either. Her ambition since early childhood had been to go into business. As she grew older it became clear that, amongst many people she knew, this was not considered an appropriate role for her, despite the frequently voiced support of her mother and father. Her disappointment at this, despite her parents' approval, fed a sense that there was injustice in the world, which was increasingly channelled into politics and how the world was governed. Unlike many people – often men – who are interested in world politics, Aditi had the remarkable talent for making connections between individual-level issues like gender discrimination and wider, structural problems. So for her it was easy to see gender bias as a problem of global governance. She had experienced it and she expected women in the UN, in big multinational corporations and in NGOs experienced it too. When she grew up, she knew she would do something about it.

In the Mason household Helen was the most vocal about Feminism, in her case very much from a Liberal point of view. What concerned her was the representation of women in decision-making bodies. Like the rest of the family she was very interested in world affairs and had become concerned with global governance as she started to realize that America could not go it alone in the world. She recognized gender, but she thought it was a hard thing to do much about. What she could get angry about was the lack of female participation and so that is what she focused on when she talked to her political representatives. She had recently joined the Junior League of New York as an outlet for her views.

John and his children tended to be somewhat passive supporters of their mother in her interest in fighting discrimination against women. For John this meant trying to avoid gender stereotyping of his children. John loved cars. A lot of the men he knew worked on their cars with their sons. John tried to resist this by working on his classic SAAB with Sofia, who had shown an interest from a very young age. This carried over into family discussion of international affairs, in which John supported Sofia's ideas about a career working in international institutions. Henry did not attack his sister's goal. He could see his parents took her ambitions seriously and Henry knew his sister would fight for her rights like his mother. This made him proud.

Problems to consider

In thinking and talking about Feminism and global governance, you might start with the following. First, is there a need for a view of global governance derived from Feminism? If there is, what is that need and how does Feminism serve it? Second, in this chapter I have referred to gender as the very essence of the approach. What is gender, how is it different from sex, and how does it serve as this core concept? Last, do you think Feminism could provide any practical guidance for reforming global governance in ways that would bring the greatest benefit to the world? In answering this question please do consider the possibility that a different way of thinking about a problem like global governance could be eminently practical in some circumstances.

Further reading

As I have made clear, not a vast amount has been published yet by Feminists on global governance. The pioneering work is an edited volume put together by Meyer and Prügl, *Gender Politics in Global Governance* (1999). Almost a decade later, Rai and Waylen edited *Global Governance: Feminist Perspectives* (2008a), which is the standard work on the approach at the time of writing and offers a good range of different views on the issue. You should read a wide selection of the chapters in this book in addition to the introduction by the editors, and chapters by Rai and Waylen. Most recently we have a specific study of the World Bank that combines political economy and gender analysis. This is Griffin's *Gendering the World Bank: Neoliberalism and the Gendered Foundations of Global Governance* (2009).

8
Rejectionism

Unlike many political concepts, the idea of global governance is still relatively new and little codified. In this context, people who talk and write about global governance often seem to ignore with impunity views about global governance that run counter to their own. This is certainly true of views that are critical of the very notion of global governance, as well as views that strongly advocate global governance. For most people, if they think about global governance at all, it is probable that what will come to mind is some mix of Institutionalism and Cosmopolitanism: a consensual and multi-lateral process conducted between states, perhaps involving NGOs, often involving some measure of leadership by the United States.

The image is positive because, as a practical reality, coop-eration is a normal feature of international relations on a day-to-day basis. North Korea and similar states are very unusual. Most states and their citizens are, when they have the opportunity, not preoccupied with waging war on each other. The normal life of international relations is in good measure one of peaceful interaction. No wonder people do not expect to encounter harsh conflict at every turn. It is not the reality of global life as they experience it. But this positive image is not universal. This chapter will consider the ideas of what I call 'Rejectionism', but which others term 'Isolation-ism' or perhaps 'nationalism': that way of thinking which is critical of the very notion of global governance, seeing in it a malign influence on political life domestically and in terms of international relations. Rejectionism has little in common with the other ways of thinking about global governance considered in this book.

Most of this discussion focuses on the US, where Rejectionism, as a critique of global governance, is most advanced. But Rejectionism could also be said to be the approach of those who reject a secular and capitalist world order, so the ideas examined in this chapter are not unique to the US.

Rejectionism may seem like an odd perspective to include in a book about global governance. But I think it essential that an interest, or even a passion, for global governance should not blind us to the reality that others not only may not share our passions and beliefs, but may indeed fail to see the benefit in what we believe in passionately. Rather than dismissing such views as those of ignorant 'rednecks', it is essential we study these reasoned views so as to understand their ideas and concerns. If nothing else, this will help us build confidence in our own views and be less afraid of challenging beliefs.

Background

Self-help has been the mantra of statesmen since the Treaty of Westphalia was signed in 1648. This treaty recognized the existence of states as opposed to kings in a break from the dynastic norms of the Middle Ages. Realism in international relations theory has enshrined this as its first principle, insisting that the rights and duties of states are paramount in international affairs, and no amount of mutual obligation or cooperation can get in the way of this reality. Some element of this conceptual history seems to be bound into Rejectionism, together with a fervent nationalism, a keen sense of the privileges and special duties of leaders, and a distrust of the ambitions of others.

This distrust of others is another feature of the Realist history, in which it is understood that all states are motivated to advance their interests by harming the interests of other states. So a focus on what I earlier called relative gains is a feature of the conceptual baggage in the background of the Rejectionist view of global governance.

Rejection of global governance and the associated post-Cold War world order is obvious and accessible in the United States. Although this may seem strange and unexpected to many non-Americans, who might assume universal American domestic support for a global governance system in which US influence is pervasive, rejection of global governance is both a mass and an elite phenomenon in the United States. It should come as no surprise that global governance has its detractors in America. There is a long history of scepticism about international entanglement in the United States, perhaps best exemplified by the Isolationist tradition that shaped US involvement in the two world wars of the twentieth century. Although the US has long been privileged as the holder of the international reserve currency, US elite resentment at the costs of maintaining a large military, when compared to allies with proportionately much smaller forces, goes back to the 1950s. In thinking about Rejectionism, we also have to reserve a place for mass opinion, often uninformed but highly consequential in democratic states. This is where the politics of nationalism, world order and leadership become pertinent to ideas about global governance.

Purpose

As we have seen in this book, people typically have different, and at times antagonistic, approaches to the concept of global governance. Institutionalism and Hegemonism have little in common. Not only do these different groups understand what the concept is quite distinctly, they vary in their understanding of the concept's use as well. This may mean they see it as a way of improving the status quo – in the case of a problem-solving approach like Institutionalism – or, more radically, they may see the concept as the basis for a transformation of the system, as in Hegemonism.

Rejectionism is quite clearly antagonistic to global governance. That antagonism is strongly felt and unmitigated.

Rejectionism sees itself as a reform movement a bit like the Tea Party movement that has developed since 2008 in the United States, determined to rekindle fundamental values and throw out many alien influences. In this sense Rejectionism represents a somewhat intolerant worldview, which is not comfortable with the same range of opinion encompassed by the other approaches to global governance.

For many who reject global governance the idea is problematic because it challenges US (or, say, Iranian) sovereign power and is a threat to US (or perhaps Syrian) interests. They tend to see global governance as a powerful orthodoxy and an established concrete reality, rather than an ideal. For them, global governance seems to represent the views of an entrenched policy establishment. The Rejectionists see themselves as outside this establishment, and are highly critical of its views about how the world should be run. On some level, it is hard not to read a fascination with conspiracy theory into Rejectionism. This is the idea that 'we' (the national state) face a plot (or many plots) against 'us' by 'them'.

Although we would normally think of transformation in different terms, perhaps as advocated by critics informed by Marxist or Cosmopolitan theory, it fits for those who oppose the idea of a global governance system. But the purpose of Rejectionism is not a tinkering with the status quo, which they see as dominated by global governance thought and practice. Their goal is transformation, although in a very different direction from that considered in the previous chapter.

Given this concern to transform, to pull apart the status quo of assumptions and policies, it seems we have to agree that Rejectionism has a critical purpose, even if that critical purpose sits at odds with other critical approaches such as Hegemonism. The way out of this problem is to characterize Rejectionism as part of the conservative wing of the critical school of global governance, incongruous as that may sound.

This purpose is utopian in character, harking back to some mythical time when the country did not need others, but stood up for itself and acted confidently. In this sense Rejectionism's agenda is nostalgic, anti-modern and fundamentally conservative. In a world of frequent crises and bewildering change, this small-town view of the world has much appeal.

Puzzles

While Institutionalism is driven by bureaucratic politics and the axioms of economic rationality, and Cosmopolitanism by a commitment to a more legitimate world, those who oppose global governance are, it seems, motivated in the first instance by an affinity with the assumptions of the Realist worldview, in which state sovereignty and self-interest are key features. The Realist world says international politics lacks any system of overarching authority. Moreover, any effort to establish one is seen by Rejectionism as a mistake in contemporary circumstances. In addition to Realist ideas about the world, ideas about the exceptional nature of the United States are central to this worldview. The US is not like other states, and has a unique history, constitution, and role in the world.

Cooperation, and how to secure it, is not the most pressing international challenge in this worldview. The key struggle is to create the conditions in which, say, traditional American values such as free enterprise and liberty can thrive, by extension improving the conditions for all global citizens. This typically means 'leadership' by the United States, which must be unconstrained from taking unilateral action where necessary. The puzzle, then, is how to secure freedom of international action for the United States.

Proponents of global governance are looking for a consensual, or at least majoritarian, process of cooperation which is not possible in the circumstances of international relations. For Rejectionists, the vital questions are always about American foreign policy, instead of global governance. What is it the United States must do in pursuit of its interests? This is best for America and the world, think the opponents of global governance.

Assuming that global governance is impossible and destructive of the state's role as agent of self-protection, further key questions for the anti-global-governance thinkers concern the origins of the impulse toward global governance. For some of the groups discussed by Rupert, this question leads to conspiratorial views and apocalyptic visions (Rupert 2000: 94–118).

Level of analysis and actors

The anti-global-governance thinkers are concerned first and foremost with sovereign states and their role in international affairs. In Rejectionism, adopting the Realist axiom, there is no enforceable overarching authority that can tell states what to do and make them do it. So, in this worldview, international relations is a wild zone lacking a lawful order, and therefore unlike the domestic communities within states. States are a bulwark for their citizens against this lawlessness. They provide what order is possible, from the bottom up. It is essential that states are able to act for this purpose, because in this worldview order cannot be created otherwise. Given this, how states work, what they do, and their actions are a key focus of analysis.

Rejectionism's focus on states includes a special concern with what goes on inside the government. Much of this seems to be driven by the outsider status of many Rejectionist commentators who see themselves as having to find and expose elite plans to entangle the state in the affairs of other national communities, undermining the state. In this sense Rejectionism seems to see government itself as the problem. Government somehow fails to represent the people effectively, and becomes a self-interested entity, only able to serve the interests of a few insiders. These insiders share little with the vast bulk of the citizenry, and seem happy to betray them to foreign powers, and to be unwilling to listen to objections.

But it is not as simple as this. Although states are the key level of analysis in Rejectionism, there is much to be feared from other levels too. Not everyone shares the Realist-sourced assumptions of Rejectionism, and threats to these ideas are perceived to come from elite interests who wish to promote global governance and from international institutions, NGOs and movements that wish to constrain or undermine state sovereignty, especially that of the United States (Bolton 2007: 441). The military is a special concern of anti-global-governance thinkers, determined as they are to preserve independent action against hostile foreign forces. There is much concern with force levels, appropriations and assessment of the relative strengths of offensive forces.

The key actor for the anti-global-governance thinkers is the United States. It is the United States that has shaped international politics decisively since the final years of the First World War. If the United States were to decide that global governance was substantial and worth pursuing, then global governance would become a meaningful policy objective, although this would be a US-dependent global governance, suggests Rejectionism.

In the anti-global-governance worldview, elite policymakers are key actors in the debate about global governance. These well-educated and well-placed thinkers are the bogeymen for the anti-global-governance movement. They advocate a globalist position, compatible with a multilateral global governance and hostile to the unilateral leadership of the United States (Bolton 2000: 206).

The mass of the population, 'the public', are key actors in this drama too. They and their sentiments seem to play the role of the innocent constantly violated and abused by others. Rejectionism appeals to the values and good habits of the public, who may be portrayed in some mythical heartland of corn fields and 'mom and pop' stores. Never mind the WalMarts and gas stations.

A sub-set of this concern with the public is an appeal to folk culture and the ways of thinking which lay claim to originating in the heartland. This nativistic sentiment may at times take the form of disparaging outsiders, incomers and those who do not belong. This is where conservatism and Rejectionism give way to less reflective and less rational thinking. But if we grant that widely held views, however irrational, can be consequential (think of witch-burning in the sixteenth century), we do have a duty to take such 'fringe' thinking seriously. Well-funded think tanks like the American Enterprise Institute, the John Birch Society, and many marginal and sometimes extreme advocates of American 'patriotic' values, including militia movements, articulate similar views. Sometimes, as Rupert documents, this descends into outright racism and xenophobia (Rupert 2000: 107).

Most recently, since the events of 11 September, the United States Government itself became an active sceptic about global governance and the interdependencies of the contemporary world, as documented by Fukuyama in his memoir on neo-conservatism in the Bush administration (Fukuyama 2006).

Assumptions

The starting assumption for the anti-global-governance think-ers is that we live in a world in which cooperation between states is difficult, to say the least. The natural inclination of most states is selfish behaviour. In these circumstances, relying on a state that has shown leadership and represents 'better' values and a resistance to tyranny is best.

In these circumstances, following the United States is the right choice for other states. But there are malevolent interests in the world, and these interests do not want to see the United States improve the world for all. These interests are quite happy with tyrannical regimes. Cosmopolitans and techno-crats play into their hands by not establishing effective defences against these interests.

Given these realities, the maintenance of a strong defence is the only option. This defence may be established in alliance with other states, but must always be capable of acting inde-pendently and without reference to others.

Ontology

Because states are assumed to be predisposed to conflict with each other in the absence of overarching authority, the ontol-ogy of the anti-global-governance thinkers inevitably starts with offensive military capabilities. International institutions and NGOs are also relevant, as sources of support for ideas about global governance.

Part of the worldview is an assumption that something very similar to the Realist notion of anarchy exists in the world. This prevailing condition shapes the necessity for self-reliance. Anti-global-governance thinkers have little faith in the regimes, norms and habits that other thinkers see as fun-damental to international interaction.

Another key issue that gets a fair amount of attention from the anti-global-governance thinkers is conspiracy. Emphasis on this varies, and is most extreme amongst the paranoid patriotic groups Rupert examined. The basic idea is that global governance is intended to frustrate and emasculate the United States, leaving the way open to enemies to replace multilateral global governance with tyranny.

Implications

The anti-global-governance worldview is clearly a negative and at times paranoid account of the possibilities of global cooperation. These characteristics may incline us to dismiss this worldview. But that would be a mistake. Although we may think the view problematic, it clearly is an influential and widely held perspective on global governance. This way of understanding the world is attractive to many – especially in the United States – stunned by the increasingly cosmopolitan character of public policy and by immigration flows. The anti-global-governance idea provides a coherent rationale for rejecting a new, different and uncertain world in which the United States does not have the final say in all international issues.

There is a dilemma in Rejectionism. Like the acquisition of nuclear weapons for defence, talking the talk of Rejectionism may provoke hostile responses that would otherwise have not existed. This movement risks stimulating precisely what it fears. In other words, by engendering fear about forces beyond the state, about a wider world we do not control, the anti-global-governance thinkers may stimulate others to think of the United States as an enemy. In other words, this approach to (or rather, against) global governance may, paradoxically, make the world a less safe place.

The broader theme is that our ways of thinking and communicating our thoughts have consequences. Rather than thinking just reflecting the world, how we think about global governance can shape what we experience, because others react to our thinking as they experience it. This phenomenon has been called performativity. It means that human thought and how we share it with others is more consequential than usually imagined. It can shape our social, economic and political circumstances, as others respond to their perception of us. Although this way of thinking reinforces some Realist notions about how the world works, the crusading or offensive character of much of the rhetoric is a real challenge to established thinking, much as fundamentalist religion challenges mainstream theology. It may provoke extreme responses in those exposed to it and in governments that have to deal with it.

Applications

Rejectionism has mostly been at some distance from the mainstream of American policy since World War II. Since the Japanese attack on Pearl Harbor on 7 December 1941, the United States has been largely willing to assume the burdens of international political leadership, even when this strained domestic politics, as during the Vietnam War, and burdened the US tax payer with high defence spending. Prior to 11 September 2001, anti-global-governance thinking contested with more internationalist thinking in American foreign-policy-making, with the latter clearly advantaged. For the most part, what we would now call Rejectionism was dominated by marginalized and extremist groups, cults, survivalists and others who celebrate a vision of a pristine Jacksonian American republic of small-holders and tradesmen. These anti-global-governance people, although significant perhaps in their own localities, were not in a position to dominate mainstream American political life.

Things changed with the destruction of the World Trade Center, and especially after the invasion of, and regime change in, Afghanistan. American policy became increasingly unilateral under the Bush administration, and although every effort was made to secure agreement from the international community, this did not prove possible – but that did not stop the subsequent invasion of Iraq in 2003. Fukuyama (2006) has suggested that neo-conservatives in the Bush White House, motivated by a grand utopian vision of bringing regime change to failed states, were able to grab policy ascendancy under the leadership of Vice-President Cheney, Paul Wolfowitz and others. This particular strand of Rejectionism, suggested Fukuyama, was not simply protective like Realism, but advocated a policy of transformation of other states. With the problems of the Doha round of trade talks, financial crisis, world recession and instances of increasing protectionism, it may be that confidence in global governance solutions is weakened. In these circumstances, hard bargaining and negotiation skills come to the fore in bilateral negotiations. Bargaining and negotiation are among the strengths of the Realist approach to international relations, and, in other spheres like economic markets, make for good business. It makes sense, perhaps, for all parties to global governance to approach international cooperation in a hard-headed way. This suggests that global governance, as a practical matter, can be measured in terms of the relative gains it provides. Relative gains are the share of the benefits (or proportion of the whole) your state receives from a negotiation. Implicit here is the idea that getting more than other states is better. The other perspective on cooperation is absolute gains. This suggests that all gain from cooperation, and it is better to be in the treaty and get something than be outside and get nothing. So bargaining is not anti-global-governance as such. However, given the depth of global governance practices and the network of institutions involved, change would have to go very far indeed before we could say that the anti-global-governance advocates had made lasting progress. Given this, the great costs of US-initiated regime change, and the observation that the US Government is a strong advocate of international treaties, it seems fair to say that Rejectionism does not dominate American policy, even if it does at times seem to be significant. It may be that the more lasting appeal of Rejectionism is in American domestic politics.

Differences of emphasis within Rejectionism

In the case of Rejectionism we can identify a substantial group of rational, if very aggressive, critics of global governance like former Ambassador John Bolton. You could, if you wished, suggest that many Realists in international relations could be seen as Rejectionists because they are dubious about the prospects for international cooperation and are advocates of a self-help approach to the global order. In addition to the respectable there are groups we could identify with Rejectionism like various forms of Christian and Islamic fundamentalism, anarchists, survivalists and militia groups – whose attitudes and behaviour have alarming qualities. Where groups advocate violence, they cross the boundary between being law-abiding – if strange – and outlaw standing. You might also include in the Rejectionism camp, if you wish, so-called 'axis of evil' states which allegedly promote terrorism as state policy, as identified by President George Bush and added to subsequently by Ambassador Bolton: Iraq (before the 2003 invasion), North Korea, Iran, Cuba, Libya (before October 2011) and Syria.

Strengths

The success of the anti-global-governance view draws great strength from the fabulous wealth and sense of opportunity in American society. This self-confidence draws from the fact that American society made itself independent from a colonial power. This history supports the idea that independence and resistance to foreign entanglements make good sense.

There is no doubt that self-reliance is a useful capacity in a world of uncertainty. Having the capability to deal with opponents and not be reliant on others has strong appeal. This strength can only have been fostered by 11 September.

A further strength of the anti-global-governance thinking is severe restriction of trust to those known well. This reduces risk and the costs of international cooperation, because it serves to limit whom regimes can include and leads to the identification of rogue states for exclusion from trust.

Weaknesses

Anti-global-governance thinkers may be underestimating the benefits of cooperation and the necessity of it in a complex and fast-developing world. By placing emphasis on distrust, they may actually create suspicion and ill-feeling.

The extreme nature of much of the rhetoric from the most fervent anti-global-governance groups is tinged with racism and xenophobia. This is clearly a weakness in terms of promoting clear, persuasive thinking about global governance and its problems.

A more subtle and ironic point is that, despite the proclamations of the anti-global-governance thinkers about the negative impact of global governance, it seems clear that the United States remains by far the most influential party in forming and implementing global governance at all levels. It is hard to avoid the conclusion that many American anti-global-governance thinkers are quixotic in their views.

Likely future development

The prospects for this conception (or anti-conception) of global governance depend very much on what happens to international cooperation in the coming years and the shape of American domestic politics. With the perceived failure of the regime-change strategy of the Bush administration, it seems likely that American policy will become more conciliatory, and therefore positive to global governance, under Obama. Failure may also stimulate a new Isolationism.

On the other hand, further domestic terrorist attacks in the United States could stimulate a new unilateralism in American politics, such as has not been seen since the Vietnam War. This environment would embolden the anti-global-governance thinkers and reshape world politics, ushering in a new age of mistrust and fear.

Overall comments

Opposition to global governance can be found both in the elite and in mass society, especially in the United States.

Drawing on self-understandings that go back to the founding of the republic, it is clear that this way of thinking is a potent force in world politics, for a time represented by some key US Government policy-makers. Although it may seem odd, this way of thinking about global governance has strong roots in established international relations theory. Where it parts company with rational thought is on the fringes, where some proponents adopt xenophobic positions.

Scenarios

We have to imagine our two families – the American Masons and the Indian Patels – very differently in what follows. Our families in these hypothetical vignettes are now convinced opponents of global governance.

Global financial crisis   It was clear to both John and Helen that the financial crisis that started in the summer of 2007 was a very major event that might well change their lives forever. They were concerned about the impact of the crisis on John's business and on their community. They were aware that other countries too were suffering from financial and economic distress. But the crisis reinforced their view that each country should take care of its own problems and that efforts to create international institutions that did the same job were a distraction at best, and very threatening to America at worst. The Masons had always been sceptics about the United Nations. Although the idea of the UN was fine, the actual practice, in their view, did not work at all. It frustrated clear decisions, it pandered to socialist states, and it hobbled the ability of the US to pursue US interests. John saw international relations much like a market. Everyone should take care of themselves. His wife Helen shared her husband's concerns. Although they were angry and embarrassed about the US banking sector, neither of them felt the US should allow global organizations a say on US policy, or bail-out other states, like those in the former Communist world in Europe or developing countries. America had more than

enough to worry about as it was. They were determined that
no US funds should be used outside the US. For John, this
meant trouble for the company who made his beloved SAAB,
but GM, like other US corporations, had to attend to US jobs
first. The kids too picked up on this sentiment in school and
were increasingly concerned about where products were
made and the need to create jobs in America for
Americans.

The Patels had long been angry about bossy international
organizations trying to tell India what to do. This they saw
as another way in which rich western countries – especially
America – tried to continue colonial relationships. But they
were not having it. Although the financial crisis was frighten-
ing, they were not going to allow India's sovereignty to be
threatened again by the IMF or the World Bank. The hostility
to these institutions amongst Agastya's friends was very
strong. They knew how important these institutions had been
in other parts of Asia, Africa and Latin America. When they
showed up, it meant prices went up, businesses closed and
there was lots of tension. Nobody wanted to make the crisis
worse with a dose of their medicine. It was for India to make
the decisions about how to deal with its problems, not
western-dominated institutions. The crisis had reinforced
family pride in India, and when the twins came home from
school with a project they had completed on India's creation
in 1947 everyone was pleased and the family enjoyed some
special food and cakes. Agastya was opposed to bailing out
debtor countries. It would be better for countries in trouble
to default on their borrowings and have the creditors face up
to the reality than to try and patch things up. Clearly there
was going to be a lot of this to come, and it was better that
countries and lenders with these problems took the hit straight
away rather than extending the nightmare over time. India
should not give money to international organizations to bail-
out defaulting debtors. India needed to look to her own
problems, as other countries should. Cooperation could be
good at times, but not if it gets in the way of each country
standing on its own two feet.

Climate change   The Masons were climate-change sceptics. If the climate was changing – and they were not clear it

was – then perhaps this was a natural process, like Rush Limbaugh said. What role humans had in it was not clear. If it was a natural process then the best thing would be for humans to adapt to the change over time as needed, as humans always had. Most of their friends felt the same way when they talked to them at the local mall or at meetings of John's Dodge Charger enthusiasts' club. They had just bought themselves a new SUV and John had changed the heads and put some new carbs on the Charger, so the last thing the Masons wanted was a lot of new environmental regulation inspired by foreign fears about a non-existent problem. They saw climate change merely as a convenient excuse for politicians to deny them their rights as American citizens. They were determined to defend their democracy against surrender to external control. Fundamentally, the Masons did not want their government negotiating treaties with other governments which bound them to change the law inside America. That seemed wrong. It meant that ordinary Americans didn't control their own laws any more. They were vocal in expressing their opposition too. John's winery made full use of every modern convenience, including poisons, and he was active with the local growers' association in defending their continued application, whatever people in Albany might want. Henry and Sofia mostly shared their parents' views. While they were happy to avoid waste – that was just good sense – they did not like the idea of their lifestyle being something decided upon in other countries. Many of their school friends agreed. If there was anything to climate change, it was for Americans to determine, not foreigners.

The Patels did not have much time for climate change. Agastya's cleaning company made use of a range of serious chemicals and he was not willing to spend more money on the environmentally friendly versions. This would make him less competitive and he was very sensitive to this issue. He had just purchased a new Mercedes for the family, and he was uninterested in a more carbon-friendly vehicle like the new Tata Nano, which seemed little more than a bicycle with a roof to him. Bhadraa had all the latest appliances in the home and they used a lot of air conditioning. They were not about to abandon these things they had worked so hard for, or the vacations they could at last afford. Agastya felt that it was for the rich countries to worry about climate change. They had had it good for a long time. They could change their lifestyles. It was for India to decide her own course and not for treaties to decide how things would be in India. India needed to keep control over Indian policy. In his view, the government should only negotiate with other governments on very few matters, where it was to India's advantage. This included telecommunications, air travel, trade and so on. It did not include matters like the climate and what to do about it. This put other countries' organizations in a position where they could force India to act, and this really was a betrayal of everything the founders of modern India had worked for during the first half of the twentieth century. Besides, given that he did not believe that global warming was an issue, putting more power in the hands of bureaucrats was just asking for trouble. These people were corrupt and incompetent and could not be trusted to act properly.

Development   John Mason had good thoughts about developing countries. The family had taken an excellent vacation in South-East Asia the previous summer and they had been impressed by the history, culture and hospitality of all the countries they visited. The family were great travellers and had done Europe, India and China in recent years. They certainly were not xenophobes or stay-at-homes. But being interested in other cultures did not mean John thought there was any role for the international community in creating economic prosperity in these places. His view was that this was a task for the locals, as it was at home for Americans. Development could not be delivered or provided. It was up to each society to do this for itself as it saw fit. This just made sense to John, as what would foreigners really know about Laos or Cambodia, and how they worked? This did not mean he was opposed to emergency aid. In fact, he gave generously when there was an earthquake or flood overseas. But 'development' seemed Orwellian to him and he did not want the United States to be part of it. Helen worried about paying tax that was sent overseas. She wanted to control how her tax money was spent and she felt she could not do that outside of America. She also preferred market solutions and was opposed to the idea that development could be planned.

The children were doing more work on foreign countries at school but John and Helen were worried by what they thought was anti-American bias on the part of their teachers, who seemed to be constantly apologizing for American actions. Both Helen and John felt American corporations had done a great deal to bring progress to developing countries, and they felt India and China were doing their best to imitate America.

Agastya Patel had seen a lot of foreign efforts to meddle in India's economic development over the years, and he was hostile to them in every form. India was for Indians. Indians would develop India as they saw fit, and no western countries or their UN agencies were going to have any influence on that process. He, like many other Indians of his age and social standing, would talk at length about the faults of foreign aid and development agencies, especially the World Bank and the IMF. He could list the problems they had made worse by their policy prescriptions in Asia, Africa and Latin America. Mr Patel was a member of the local business association. This club, which a relative of Mr Patel's had founded in the 1970s, met in what had been a club for white members of the British Raj in the heyday of British India. Agastya always felt slightly uneasy walking into this place. The association frequently discussed their need for better sanitation and energy infrastructure in Bangalore. But they saw this as something that their taxes should pay for and good Indian engineers should design and build. Bhadraa was concerned about the state of other countries in South Asia not growing as fast as India. What could India do to prevent periodic refugee crises from Bangladesh, for instance, when the floods came? She debated these more enduring issues with her husband from time to time, but she too was very wary of western-dominated NGOs and international organizations who thought they knew better and often ended up making things worse. The children, as always, were quite nationalistic about the matter. They were proud that India was developing fast and they were especially happy that the country was doing this on its own terms.

Security John Mason was in many respects a hawk. He had served in the first Gulf War as a junior officer in command of an M1 Abrams tank and he was still a Major in his local National Guard unit, although he was now an artillery man or gunner, rather than a tankie. He did not think of himself as reckless by any means, but he took seriously President Bush's idea that pre-emptive action might be necessary and was America's right if the country was threatened. He knew that in war all bets are off. An old commander of his, Major Shue, had told him when he was a very junior cadet that, no matter what it said in the field manual about the rules of war, as soon as it kicks off you can be sure the US military will fire white phosphorous rounds from their tanks and artillery. This experience meant that when it came to security John had no time for multilateral or mutual arrangements, unless they were alliances. States and their allies have to look after themselves. As far as he was concerned, you could not rely on others to enforce your own security. Indeed, to do so was to expect too much of other states, who must be mindful of their own problems. Helen and the children had always been respectful of John's military service even when this caused Helen great anguish, as it had in 1991. Henry expected to serve in the Guard himself when he was old enough, and Sofia was interested in becoming a military pilot. Unlike other families, who find aviation security a nuisance in the era following 9/11, this family never complained. Although they too shared the feeling that things had not gone right in Iraq, they did not abandon the Bush doctrine of pre-emption.

Although the Patels were not a military family like the Masons, they were very aware of security because of the history of conflict with India's neighbours and the real threat of domestic terrorism. War with Pakistan in particular had shaped attitudes to security in contemporary India. This experience gave the family, like many other Indian families, a certain stoic character in the eyes of non-Indians. But this did not mask a great anger at the outrages they had witnessed. Although not normally one to agree with higher taxes, Agastya was eager to see the Indian armed forces equipped with the best weapons after many years of making do with old and outdated technology. It was about time, in his view, that India improved the training and equipment of domestic security forces to international standards. Many of these troops were still using bolt-action rifles manufactured during World War II. What sort of response could such soldiers offer to terrorists with AK-47s and C4 explosives? The Patels were firm supporters of Indian non-alliance. This policy had served India well for decades and forced India to be self-reliant. For a new nation this was a good thing, as relying on the former colonial power would have been all too easy but would have retarded meaningful Indian sovereignty. India's independent nuclear deterrent was a matter of frequent discussion in their household. Bhadraa had memories of watching documentaries about the victims of Hiroshima and Nagasaki and so was concerned about the vast destructive power of nuclear weapons. Her children could barely conceive of the 'nukes, but knew they made India a much bigger and more important country than she would have been otherwise. Agastya acknowledged that nuclear weapons are truly terrible things. But in his view India needs these weapons to ensure that India retains sovereignty in a world of great uncertainty.

Gender relations   John Mason was something of a conservative. Although he was no redneck he did like fast cars, messing around with engines and drinking cheap beer. In this he was pretty average amongst his group of friends. He and Helen had always had a good partnership, but it was fairly traditional. He made most of the money and she took care of things at home. This seemed to work for them, or at least it had so far. There were no signs of Henry or Sofia moving away from these ideas. But it was early days and they had a lot of growing up to do yet. John was horrified by some of the images they saw on TV about what had happened to women in Iraq and Afghanistan since regime change there. Helen felt very strongly about these things too, and they knew people who supported the continuing fight in both countries partly in opposition to the subordination of women there. However, while the Masons were willing to support regime change in US interests, they defined gender relations and the rights of women as matters of internal, domestic policy, and not things properly belonging to international relations. They were uncomfortable with such matters being politicized in the first place. Given this, they were hostile in principle to international organizations and NGOs focusing on gender relations and the rights of women, because such matters were properly national issues for sovereign governments and their citizens. They could see the merits of a more 'ground up' approach to the development of gender relations through micro-finance lending to women in developing countries, although this should be financed through the local banks and capital markets, in their view, and not through foreign aid. Gender relations were not, in their opinion, an area for concerted policy.

Women's issues were something Agastya Patel tended to avoid discussing inside the family. He was rather traditional and quite happy for his wife to assume all the domestic chores while he attended to his business. Bhadraa saw this as a choice she had made in the interests of her children. But this did not mean she was uninterested in women's rights. She was passionately concerned with these matters because she knew that many women did not have the ability to make choices as she did. Where Agastya and Bhadraa came together was in their opposition to interference in domestic life by western NGOs. It was something both of them had remarked on from time to time and a great irritation to them. Agastya had recently been written to by a foreign-based NGO about the conditions of work for his female employees. He had torn the letter up and thrown it away. It was not that he was hostile to his female employees. It was just that he considered being approached like this to be interference by foreign busybodies, which he was determined to resist. Bhadraa had been involved in volunteering in the worst parts of Bangalore. She had been disappointed by how some of the western women spoke to Indian women. 'They were so patronising, Agastya, you wouldn't believe it. I felt ashamed to be Indian', she said. When Bhadraa had reproached the western women, they were able to talk about the issue constructively, which was a pleasing outcome for Mrs Patel. Agastya saw the incident as part of a process he had been battling all his life, in which outside 'experts' from rich countries thought they knew best and endeavoured to tell Indians, and people in many other developing countries, how to live.

Problems to consider

In thinking and talking about Rejectionism and global governance, you might start with the following. First, is this a serious perspective on global governance at all, given the implacable hostility to international cooperation evident here? In other words, should Rejectionism be in a book on perspectives on global governance? Second, what criteria do you use to identify non-US Rejectionists? After all, there is no shortage of critics of US foreign policy. How can we distinguish criticism of the US and Rejectionism from each other? Last, at what point does Rejectionism cease to be a serious position on global governance and potentially merge into criminality? In other words, how far can you go before your opposition to policy ceases to be an acceptable stance and borders on law-breaking? How do we know?

Further reading

The internet is awash with Rejectionism, as is Talk Radio and the Fox News network in the United States. Books by the likes of Glenn Beck are popular. Bolton's *Surrender is Not an Option: Defending America at the United Nations and Abroad* (2007) is informative and a good account of this position. The reader should also consult John J. Mearsheimer's 2002 volume, *The Tragedy of Great Power Politics*. Mearsheimer's book is an elegant and powerful statement of 'offensive Realism', arguing a case for US hegemony. I include this thoughtful and learned book here because the case it makes for self-reliance – indeed, for hegemony – is cogent and not at all subject to the sort of criticism we might want to direct at less reasoned examples of Rejectionism.

9
Conclusions

The head-long rush toward what for many seems a globalized society has raised uncertainties and opportunities for governance (or chaos) which both incorporate and transcend the nation-state that dominated the development of the modern world. States remain central actors in the world of global governance, but their claim to primacy is challenged even in traditional spheres like security. This is an exciting transition, around which a new concept called global governance has started to develop. This seems to be about problems that transcend the narrow limits of national states. However, there is no widely shared understanding of global governance. Different groups have competing ideas, with diverging assumptions and implications. The purpose of this book has been to identify some of the most interesting ideas and examine them so the reader can make more informed judgements about conceptions of global governance. After a few paragraphs in which I discuss the book's prior chapters, I ask a series of quite provocative questions about global governance and the prospects for the concept and its realization. If you do not want to read again about prior chapters I suggest you skip ahead to the questions.

In chapters 3 to 8, I addressed, respectively, Institutionalism (chapter 3), Transnationalism (chapter 4), Cosmopolitanism (chapter 5), what I call Hegemonism (chapter 6), Feminism (chapter 7) and what I have termed, for want of a better word, Rejectionism (chapter 8). In each chapter I tried to tease out the implications of the respective way of thinking, as well as its sense of what matters and what does not. In doing this I allowed myself to be informed by scholarly writings, but I did not limit the universe of thinking about global governance to the thoughts of scholars, as this would be to exaggerate the codification of global governance thinking as it actually exists. I evaluated strengths and weaknesses and attempted to provide some sense of the future development of each concept. I tried to carry out this explication in as systematic and methodical a way as possible within the limits of a concise volume such as this. The hypothetical vignettes involving the Mason and Patel families helped, I hope, to illustrate the differences in views and the concrete implications of these differences. Concreteness, in the context of a debate about ideas, is advantageous to understanding. I chose to focus on topical problems most of us will have some familiarity with: the global financial crisis, climate change, development, security and gender relations. This element of each chapter has a narrative quality to it, and intentionally so. Global governance is usually debated in abstract terms, and some of that is evident in this book too. But global governance is very much a problem of concern to us all as citizens of the world. Making the problem of global governance meaningful and relevant is essential.

The success or failure of these different ways of thinking about global governance is going to depend on what happens in the world. If trade remains free and open, all but the anti-global-governance perspective, or what I have called Rejectionism, will be bolstered. If the world descends into greater conflict, geo-political rivalry or distrust, perhaps because of unexpected war – say, between China and Taiwan, or Iran and the West – then it is likely that all this talk about global governance will be muted, at least until the horrors of such an event are through being visited upon us once again. But events do not control us in this simple unequivocal way. People can build a better world themselves by debating and reaching toward something more satisfactory that meets their needs. Leadership and constructive dialogue are possible and necessary if we wish to transcend the limits on our cooperation created by others.

In this book I have argued that the impetus behind the debate about global governance has its origins in the policy world. Global governance here is a limited managerial view of the world. This is in large part a reaction to the failure of prior programmes for global change, as I argued in chapter 2. These managerial underpinnings limit the concept of global governance and shape the concept's political implications. The managerial origins of global governance do not prevent more radical perspectives from offering alternative views but they undermine the claims of these other views, such as Cosmopolitanism and Hegemonism. Global governance, while a recognition of new phenomena like globalization, is not, as a way of thinking, so very new itself. The impulse to cooperation is not novel in global affairs. It remains limited and partial, rather than system-changing. So it seems that, contrary to the excitement about the newness of global governance, the real story about this concept is one of continuity. Global governance is the new language and conceptual universe in which our policy-makers, activists and scholars have learnt to debate the nature and extent of the world's problems and how they can be alleviated. Novelty can be found in the new challenges to global cooperation. Global governance provides the opportunity for a debate about how to deal with the world's problems in the context of globalization. In this sense, chapters 3 to 8 represent different tendencies in a debate about which approach will dominate policy in the years to come.

Is global governance actually a useful concept? Thinking about the possibility and reality of global governance forces us to consider the problems that motivate the exercising of authority, and the challenges which make some forms more effective than others. Although highly contested, the idea of global governance, as something above and beyond the national state, forces us to consider what would make global governance work and what would prevent it from working. So the concept may provide the means to think through political systems at the highest level in our world. To put the concept on the table is useful in another sense. The notion of anarchy, or an absence of authority over and above states, became a common denominator of much Cold-War theorizing about international relations. To talk about global governance, however it is conceived, does seem to me to challenge this unspoken assumption. That, I think, is a positive development and makes global governance potentially very useful. Finally, in a world where knowledge is more important than ever, it makes a lot of sense to recast global power relations not in terms of a conspiracy but in terms of the primarily consensual elements. World order will continue to be underpinned by coercion, no doubt, but it seems clear that the balance has moved from more coercion to more consent, and that makes global governance – as opposed to a global empire, say – much more likely and relevant to the politics we are going to witness in coming decades.

What could destroy global governance? Achieving a unified view of what global governance is and what it should be is beyond the scope of this book. My expectation is that a diversity of views is normal and will in all probability persist in the absence of a major world war, famine or uncontrollable economic crisis. Differences of views are not in themselves unexpected. What could bust apart globalization, the rise of alternative nodes of authority and governance, and international cooperation over transboundary issues is the rise of one or more unsatisfied powers, as occurred in the 1930s in the wake of World War I, the Treaty of Versailles and the Great Depression. At that time, in a story we know well, a number of states who were to go on to form the Axis powers in World War II sought territorial enlargement on a grand scale in Europe and Asia. Although a repeat of this experience seems unlikely, there are many regional powers with considerable ambition who might pose a threat to world order. Another way to think about this issue is to consider the desire on the part of established and historically influential states to retain this role, even in the context of newly emergent and more vibrant states in South America, Asia and perhaps the Middle East. A potential clash between those on the rise and those facing relative decline is conceivable. A rational person would say both sides have a strong interest in maintaining cooperation and ensuring the continuance – and indeed the expansion – of governance over global issues. But this was the situation prior to August 1914 too.

What could corrupt global governance? Can we imagine a situation in which global governance suffers a loss of legitimacy and comes to be viewed as no more than a new tyranny? Some readings of Hegemonism and Rejectionism would suggest this is the situation we already face, of course. Cynicism about global governance might set in if there is no tangible action on transborder problems when those problems are acute. An example would be unilateral selfish action by states in the face of renewed financial crisis, making the crisis worse. This is a not-inconceivable scenario and elements of this occurred in the crisis that began in 2007, specifically when the Irish Government guaranteed all bank deposits. If global governance is no use in acute situations like this and is readily discarded, then what use is it? The perception of corruption might also set in, as perhaps is already the case with the European Union, if collective action in the name of global governance comes to be seen as something shrouded in red tape and as a source of contracts and pork for private corporations and local politicians. Bail-outs to failing financial institutions might provoke a strong negative reaction. In other words, global governance might become just another system in which unelected officialdom extracts rents from the populace with little perceived tangible benefit in return. Rejectionism is already deeply sceptical about the work of the United Nations system.

Is there a democratic deficit in global governance? Mainstream conceptions of global governance, such as Institutionalism, do not offer any direct link between individuals and global governance institutions. We are left to infer that the democratic mandate for international institutions comes from their relationship with national states. Many international relations scholars with sympathies for the Realist position, which sees states as the primary actor in world politics, would happily endorse this model. But is this line of thought actually likely to undermine global governance? If skilful individuals feel themselves increasingly willing to assert their rights, given their human capital and the reorientation of productive life around knowledge, then it seems likely that the idea that global governance acquires its legitimacy purely through states is going to become increasingly problematic. Some form of direct representation could become necessary to avoid dissatisfaction compromising international cooperation on transboundary issues. Another situation in which a democratic deficit might undermine global governance is when private agencies exercise a lot of governance, but are not accountable. A classic example is credit rating agencies and their ability, especially in the indebted developed world, to exercise considerable perceived coercion when it comes to the possibility of downgrading a corporation or a national government. Nobody elected the rating agencies, and their activities, and the work of NGOs that set themselves up to address particular problems, are free of the constraints of most public institutions. If globalization does mean an increasing scope for privately sourced global governance, as the Commission on Global Governance wants, this issue will have to be justified or otherwise resolved – perhaps, as in the case of the rating agencies, with the aid of some sort of public body acting as a clearing house.

Who should global governance be for? Robert Cox has suggested that all theory is for a purpose and for some interest. There is no such thing – in the social world at least – as disinterested or neutral knowledge apart from its link to social forces. If that is so – and we should acknowledge that many would dispute this notion – what are the implications? One interpretation is that global governance can simply never be coherent or effective because the knowledge underpinning it must always be partial, and therefore the governance it produces must also be limited. Another view would be that global governance should be driven by expertise, and that citizens should defer to experts as these people are best placed to tell the mass of the populace what specific policies should be enacted. This is an elitist view and perhaps what has actually happened in most institutions of global governance on a daily basis. Another approach – and, I suspect, the approach Cox favours – is to ask: who are the dispossessed now and who stand to benefit most from assuming leadership of global governance? The answer to this question, from the Hegemonist point of view, is likely to be the large majority of the population. Curiously, this seems to be a position much of Rejectionism would be comfortable with, starting as it does with a sense that an arrogant elite have taken upon themselves the making of all major policy decisions about international affairs.

How will the idea of global governance change in future? One of the things we can be sure of is that the challenges we face and the ideas we use to meet those challenges will not remain the same. Let us consider three scenarios. In the first scenario, the broad parameters of our world order remain unchanged. The rich countries remain rich, crises abate, and the new rising powers run into a brick wall of flat productivity and their growth peters out. In this scenario, we can expect the emphasis to be on continuity, on getting back to the 'normal' order of things as quickly as possible. What this amounts to is an emphasis on market institutions and the sort of finance-centred system of production that has emerged in the West since the end of the Bretton Woods regime. Global governance will likely remain not much more than a new name for international institutions, although private agencies will increasingly take over functions formerly undertaken by large public bodies. In the second scenario, the rich world remains mired in slow growth, unemployment and weak self-confidence indefinitely, as Japan has since the early 1990s. The newly emerging powers start to assert themselves, but instead of seeking emancipation for all are content to replace their former overlords with themselves. Global governance, although now more diverse, remains far less than Cosmopolitanism might wish it to be. In the third scenario, perhaps the most interesting, the challenge of continuing to live well on our planet gives rise to a 'learning process', perhaps through a crisis or series of reversals. This would be similar to Polanyi's 'great transformation', in which society subsumes the market after similar systemic problems. In this scenario, global society would start to emerge and address some of the problems I have referred to in this book. Unlike the first two scenarios, the third involves a clear change in identity of the key units in the system, and the emergence of a new system to support global governance – a nascent global society. This leads to a secular shift in the dominant worldview toward a more cooperative and sustainable mode of life.

Can we imagine a future without global governance? One possible future, of course, is for us to move from a well-developed system of global governance to one of global government. But in the absence of an extra-planetary threat from marauding comets or malevolent aliens, this really does seem just a long-term possibility. It does seem hard to anticipate, given globalization and technological change, that challenges that span the planet will somehow disappear, even if capitalism were to end next Tuesday. I certainly hope, as I am sure you do too, that we will get better at dealing with these problems. This might mean that the challenges of global governance and the capacity to respond to planet-spanning threats simply become normal. So global governance does not disappear as such, but it might become part of our everyday way of doing things, and so merge into the infrastructure of our lives, much as we have come to be able to depend on reliable electric power and decent roads, at least in the developed world.

Is there a good future for global governance and should we be excited about the concept, variously understood? At the start of this chapter, I pointed squarely to continuity when thinking about global governance. Given this, you might assume I think there is little to get excited about here. One of the consistent themes anyone who studies international relations for any period of time has to get used to is the notion coming from the Realist camp that anarchy forces states to be narrowly self-regarding, and limits any hope of substantial cooperation between states in the world. After all, aren't they just trying to get the better of each other? The funny thing is that, despite this claim, made over and over again in the literature and present in movies and popular culture (Walter Matthau's speech in *Fail-Safe* comes to mind), the reality of world politics is quite different. In that world, states cooperate with each other, day in and day out. You couldn't make an international phone call or mail a letter to your cousin in Australia if cooperation was as rare and unlikely a phenomenon as suggested. What global governance does, despite the latent agenda to limit the concept to managerial ambitions that I have identified, is to highlight this cooperation and, importantly, provide us all with an opportunity to make cooperation more of a reality by acting on that cooperation collectively. In this intersubjective sense of agency derived from the thinking of John Searle, we can, if enough of us want it to be so, assume global governance is a foundation stone of international affairs. By acting collectively as if global governance (of the sort we want) is a fact, we can make global governance a reality that powerful agents cannot ignore. This sort of mobilization and transformation is what the Arab spring was about, and this demonstrated the potential for change latent within global governance. That is something to get excited about!

Toward the end of each chapter in this book, I incorporated some special discussion. In the tradition of counterfactual analysis in the social sciences, which encourages us to imagine alternative realities if prior conditions were different, each of the substantive chapters used scenarios or historical vignettes in which the Patels and Masons adopted the broad outline assumptions of each perspective on global governance, conditioned by their different circumstances, as presented in successive chapters, as a way to bring home the meaning and significance of each view of global governance. At the end of this tour of some of the key perspectives on global governance, let us reconsider the prototypical Mason family of Suffolk County, Long Island, NY, and the Patels of Bangalore, India. Most people are so preoccupied by their own concerns and problems that the wider world around them and how it works rarely get seriously considered. But with globalization, financial crisis and environmental phenomena like climate change, that neat, domestic world feels increasingly vulnerable to dislocation. So, like you and billions similar to you, the Masons and the Patels think and take action themselves. Although they are less connected to political parties in all the scenarios than were the previous generation, they are much more connected to changing the politics of their everyday lives through their consumption choices, their means of transportation and even their ambitions. Global governance may not only be about states taking cooperative action, as envisaged by Institutionalism. Instead, it may be that problems, crises and injustice also drive change from the bottom up. This transformation in the capacity and attitudes of the individual is significant. People, even those who have endured tyranny in some places for decades, seem increasingly willing – and, perhaps more importantly, able – to assert themselves using social media against what were once considered to be the immovable structures of the state. Other things being equal, the approach to global governance that can work with the changing capacity and identity of individuals is the one that will be successful. This new assertiveness means that national governments, which remain a key variable in creating and maintaining any semblance of global governance, must become more adaptive themselves if they are to remain relevant and useful to families like the Masons and Patels. If states manage to change their form to become more responsive and accountable, they can rebuild and maintain their role in a world of transglobal challenges. If states are unable to adapt to this world, it is likely a long period of institutional change will be generated, moving authority both downward and perhaps upward from the national state. The Masons and Patels will watch with keen interest.

Bibliography

Allison, G., and P. Zelikow. 1999. *Essence of Decision: Explaining the Cuban Missile Crisis*. 2nd edition. London: Longman.

Avant, D. D., M. Finnemore and S. K. Sell (eds.). 2010. *Who Governs the Globe?* Cambridge: Cambridge University Press.

Barnett, M., and R. Duvall. 2005. 'Power in International Politics'. *International Organization*. 59, Winter: 39–75.

Barnett, M., and M. Finnemore. 2004. *Rules for the World: International Organizations in Global Politics*. Ithaca, NY: Cornell University Press.

Barnett, M., and T. G. Weiss (eds.). 2008. *Humanitarianism in Question: Politics, Power, Ethics*. Ithaca, NY, and London: Cornell University Press.

Beck, U. 1992. *Risk Society: Towards a New Modernity*. London: Sage.

Bieler, A. 2006. *The Struggle for a Social Europe: Trade Unions and EMU in Times of Global Restructuring*. Manchester: Manchester University Press.

Bjola, C., and M. Kornprobst (eds.). 2010. *Arguing Global Governance: Agency, Lifeworld and Shared Reasoning*. London: Routledge.

Bolton, J. R. 2000. 'Should We Take Global Governance Seriously?' *Chicago Journal of International Law*: 205–21.

Bolton, J. R. 2007. *Surrender is Not an Option: Defending America at the United Nations and Abroad*. New York: Threshold Editions.

Bundy, Harvey H. 1947. 'An Introductory Note'. *International Organization*. 1, February: 1–2.

Burnham, P. 1999. 'The Politics of Economic Management in the 1990s'. *New Political Economy*. 4, 1, March: 37–54.

Carter, N. 2010. 'Climate Change and the Politics of the Global Environment' in M. Beeson and N. Bisley (eds.) *Issues in 21st Century World Politics*. Basingstoke: Palgrave Macmillan.

Chang, H.-J., and I. Grabel. 2004. *Reclaiming Development: An Alternative Economic Policy Manual*. London: Zed Books.

Chwieroth, J. M. 2009. *Capital Ideas: The IMF and the Rise of Financial Liberalization*. Princeton, NJ: Princeton University Press.

Claude, Jr, Inis L. 1971. *Swords into Ploughshares: The Problems and Progress of International Organization*. 4th edition. New York: Random House.

Commission on Global Governance. 1995. *Our Global Neighborhood: The Report of the Commission on Global Governance*. Oxford: Oxford University Press.

Cox, R. W. 1987. *Production, Power, and World Order: Social Forces in the Making of History*. New York: Columbia University Press.

Cox, R. W., and H. K. Jacobson. 1973. *The Anatomy of Influence: Decision Making in International Organization*. New Haven: Yale University Press.

Cox, R. W., with T. J. Sinclair. 1996. *Approaches to World Order*. Cambridge: Cambridge University Press.

Dasgupta, P. 2007. *Economics: A Very Short Introduction*. Oxford: Oxford University Press.

Della Porta, D., M. Andretta, L. Mosca and H. Reiter. 2006. *Globalization from Below: Transnational Activists and Protest Networks*. Minneapolis: University of Minnesota Press.

Diehl, P. F., and B. Frederking (eds.). 2010. *The Politics of Global Governance: International Organizations in an Interdependent World*. 4th edition. Boulder, CO: Lynne Rienner.

Dingwerth, K., and P. Pattberg. 2006. 'Global Governance as a Perspective on World Politics'. *Global Governance*. 12: 185–203.

Drezner, D. W. 2007. *All Politics is Global: Explaining International Regulatory Regimes*. Princeton, NJ: Princeton University Press.

Dryzek, J. S. 2010. *Foundations and Frontiers of Deliberative Governance*. Oxford: Oxford University Press.

Ellickson, R. C. 1991. *Order without Law: How Neighbors Settle Disputes*. Cambridge, MA: Harvard University Press.

Enloe, C. 2001. *Bananas, Beaches and Bases: Making Feminist Sense of International Politics*. 2nd edition. Berkeley, CA: University of California Press.

Ferguson, N. 1999. 'Introduction' in N. Ferguson (ed.) *Virtual History: Alternatives and Counterfactuals*. New York: Basic Books.

Frieden, J. A., D. A. Lake and K. A. Schultz. 2010. *World Politics: Interests, Interactions, Institutions*. New York: Norton.

Friedman, R. B. 1990. 'On the Concept of Authority in Political Philosophy' in J. Raz (ed.) *Authority*. New York: New York University Press.

Fukuyama, F. 1992. *The End of History and the Last Man*. Boston: Free Press.

Fukuyama, F. 2006. *After the Neocons: America at the Crossroads*. London: Profile Books. Published in the United States as *America at the Crossroads: Democracy, Power, and the Neoconservative Legacy*.

Gamble, A. 2009. *The Spectre at the Feast: Capitalist Crisis and the Politics of Recession*. Basingstoke: Palgrave Macmillan.

Germain, R. D. 1997. *The International Organization of Credit: States and Global Finance in the World-Economy*. Cambridge: Cambridge University Press.

Germain, R. 2010. *Global Politics & Financial Governance*. Basingstoke: Palgrave Macmillan.

Giddens, A. 1998. *The Third Way: The Renewal of Social Democracy*. Cambridge: Polity Press.

Gill, S. 1990. *American Hegemony and the Trilateral Commission*. Cambridge: Cambridge University Press.

Gill, S. 2008. *Power and Resistance in the New World Order*. 2nd edition. Basingstoke: Palgrave Macmillan.

Goldstein, J., and R. O. Keohane (eds.). 1993. *Ideas and Foreign Policy: Beliefs, Institutions and Political Change*. Ithaca, NY, and London: Cornell University Press.

Griffin, P. 2006. 'The World Bank'. *New Political Economy*. 11, 4: 571–81.

Griffin, P. 2009. *Gendering the World Bank: Neoliberalism and the Gendered Foundations of Global Governance*. Basingstoke: Palgrave Macmillan.

Hall, R. B. 2008. *Central Banking as Global Governance: Constructing Financial Credibility*. Cambridge: Cambridge University Press.

Harrod, J. 1987. *Power, Production, and the Unprotected Worker*. New York: Columbia University Press.

Harrod, J. and R. O'Brien (eds.). 2002. *Global Unions? Theory and Strategy of Organized Labour in the Global Political Economy*. London: Routledge.

Hawkins, D. G., D. A. Lake, D. L. Nielson and M. J. Tierney (eds.). 2006. *Delegation and Agency in International Organizations.* Cambridge: Cambridge University Press.

Hay, C. 2007. *Why We Hate Politics.* Oxford: Blackwell.

Held, D. 1995. *Democracy and the Global Order: From the Modern State to Cosmopolitan Governance.* Cambridge: Polity Press.

Held, D. 2004. *Global Covenant: The Social Democratic Alternative to the Washington Consensus.* Cambridge: Polity Press.

Held, D. 2006. 'Reframing Global Governance: Apocalypse Soon or Reform!' *New Political Economy.* 11, 2: 157–76.

Held, D. 2010. *Cosmopolitanism: Ideals and Realities.* Cambridge: Polity Press.

Held, D., and M. Koenig-Archibugi. 2003. *Taming Globalization: Frontiers of Governance.* Cambridge: Polity Press.

Held, D., A. McGrew, D. Goldblatt and J. Perraton. 1999. *Global Transformations: Politics, Economics and Culture.* Stanford: Stanford University Press.

Hewson, M. 2005. 'The UN after Sixty Years: Progress or Recurrence?' *Journal of Military and Strategic Studies.* 7, 5, September: 1–38.

Hewson, M. 2008. 'Modes of Global Governance: A Long-Term Perspective'. *The Global Studies Journal.* 1, 1: 1–8.

Hewson, M., and T. J. Sinclair (eds.). 1999. *Approaches to Global Governance Theory.* Albany, NY: State University of New York Press.

Higgott, R. 2010. 'Governing the Global Economy: Multilateral Economic Institutions' in M. Beeson and N. Bisley (eds.) *Issues in 21st Century World Politics.* Basingstoke: Palgrave Macmillan.

Higgott, R., and E. Erman. 2010. 'Deliberative Global Governance and the Question of Legitimacy: What Can We Learn from the WTO?' *Review of International Studies.* 36: 449–70.

Hobson, J. M. 2007. 'Is Critical Theory Always for the White West and for Western Imperialism? Beyond Westphilian Towards a Post-Racist Critical IR'. *Review of International Political Economy.* 33: 91–116.

Hobson, J. M., and L. Seabrooke (eds.). 2007. *Everyday Politics of the World Economy.* Cambridge: Cambridge University Press.

Hoskyns, C. 2008. 'Governing the EU: Gender and Macroeconomics' in S. M. Rai and G. Waylen (eds.) *Global Governance: Feminist Perspectives.* Basingstoke: Palgrave Macmillan.

Karns, M. P., and K. A. Mingst. 2009. *International Organizations: The Politics and Processes of Global Governance.* 2nd edition. Boulder, CO: Lynne Rienner.

Keck, M. E., and K. Sikkink. 1998. *Activists Beyond Borders: Advocacy Networks in International Politics*. Ithaca, NY, and London: Cornell University Press.

Keohane, R. O. 1984. *After Hegemony: Cooperation and Discord in the World Political Economy*. Princeton, NJ: Princeton University Press.

Keohane, R. O., and J. S. Nye. 1977. *Power and Interdependence: World Politics in Transition*. Boston: Little, Brown.

Kjaer, A. M. 2004. *Governance*. Cambridge: Polity Press.

Klotz, A. 1995. *Norms in International Relations: The Struggle against Apartheid*. Ithaca, NY, and London: Cornell University Press.

Koenig-Archibugi, M. 2003. 'Introduction: Globalization and the Challenge to Governance' in D. Held and M. Koenig-Archibugi, *Taming Globalization: Frontiers of Governance*. Cambridge: Polity Press.

Koppell, J. G. S. 2010. *World Rule: Accountability, Legitimacy, and the Design of Global Governance*. Chicago: University of Chicago Press.

Koremenos, B., C. Lipson and D. Snidal (eds.). 2004. *The Rational Design of International Institutions*. Cambridge: Cambridge University Press.

Lenin, V. I. 1970 [1917]. *Imperialism: The Highest Stage of Capitalism*. Moscow: Progress Publishers.

Lukes, S. 1986. 'Introduction' in S. Lukes (ed.) *Power*. New York: New York University Press.

Mearsheimer, J. J. 2002. *The Tragedy of Great Power Politics*. New York: Norton.

Meyer, M. K., and E. Prügl (eds.). 1999. *Gender Politics in Global Governance*. New York: Rowman & Littlefield.

Mills, C. W. 1956. *The Power Elite*. New York: Oxford University Press.

Mittelman, J. H. 2000. *The Globalization Syndrome: Transformation and Resistance*. Princeton, NJ: Princeton University Press.

Mittelman, J. H. 2004. *Whither Globalization? The Vortex of Knowledge and Ideology*. London: Routledge.

Mittelman, J. H. 2010. *Hyperconflict: Globalization and Insecurity*. Palo Alto, CA: Stanford University Press.

Murphy, C. N. 1994. *International Organization and Industrial Change: Global Governance since 1850*. Cambridge: Polity Press.

Murphy, C. N. 2000. 'Global Governance: Poorly Done and Poorly Understood'. *International Affairs*. 76, 4: 789–803.

Murphy, C. N. 2005. *Global Institutions, Marginalization, and Development*. London: Routledge.

O'Brien, R., A. M. Goetz, J. A. Scholte and M. Williams. 2000. *Contesting Global Governance: Multilateral Economic Institutions and Global Social Movements*. Cambridge: Cambridge University Press.

Ostrom, E. 1990. *Governing the Commons: The Evolution of Institutions for Collective Action*. Cambridge: Cambridge University Press.

Payne, A. and N. Phillips. 2010. *Development*. Cambridge: Polity Press.

Persaud, R. B. 2001. *Counter-Hegemony and Foreign Policy: The Dialectics of Marginalized and Global Forces in Jamaica*. Albany, NY: State University of New York Press.

Polanyi, K. 1957 [1944]. *The Great Transformation: Political and Economic Origins of Our Time*. Boston: Beacon Press.

Rai, S. M., and G. Waylen (eds.). 2008a. *Global Governance: Feminist Perspectives*. Basingstoke: Palgrave Macmillan.

Rai, S. M., and G. Waylen. 2008b. 'Introduction: Feminist Perspectives on Analysing and Transforming Global Governance' in S. M. Rai and G. Waylen (eds.) *Global Governance: Feminist Perspectives*. Basingstoke: Palgrave Macmillan.

Reus-Smit, C. 2004. *The Politics of International Law*. Cambridge: Cambridge University Press.

Rhoads, S. E. 1985. *The Economist's View of the World: Government, Markets, & Public Policy*. Cambridge: Cambridge University Press.

Risse, T., S. C. Ropp and K. Sikkink (eds.). 1999. *The Power of Human Rights: International Norms and Domestic Change*. Cambridge: Cambridge University Press.

Risse-Kappen, T. (ed.). 1995. *Bringing Transnational Relations Back In: Non-State Actors, Domestic Structures and International Institutions*. Cambridge: Cambridge University Press.

Rosenau, J. N. 1990. *Turbulence in World Politics: A Theory of Change and Continuity*. Princeton, NJ: Princeton University Press.

Rosenau, J. N. 1992. 'Governance, Order, and Change in World Politics' in J. N. Rosenau and E.-O. Czempiel (eds.) *Governance without Government: Order and Change in World Politics*. Cambridge: Cambridge University Press.

Rosenau, J. N. 1997. *Along the Domestic–Foreign Frontier: Exploring Governance in a Turbulent World*. Cambridge: Cambridge University Press.

Rosenau, J. N. 2003. *Distant Proximities: Dynamics Beyond Globalization*. Princeton, NJ: Princeton University Press.

Rosenau, J. N., and E.-O. Czempiel (eds.). 1992. *Governance without Government: Order and Change in World Politics.* Cambridge: Cambridge University Press.

Rupert, M. 2000. *Ideologies of Globalization: Contending Visions of a New World Order.* London: Routledge.

Sassen, S. 1998. *Globalization and its Discontents: Essays on the New Mobility of People and Money.* New York: The New Press.

Schechter, M. G. 1999. 'Our Global Neighborhood: Pushing Problem-Solving Theory to Its Limits and the Limits of Problem-Solving Theory' in M. Hewson and T. J. Sinclair (eds.) *Approaches to Global Governance Theory.* Albany, NY: State University of New York Press.

Scholte, J. A. 2005. *Globalization: A Critical Introduction.* 2nd edition. Basingstoke: Palgrave Macmillan.

Scholte, J. A. 2011. 'Global Governance, Accountability and Civil Society' in J. A. Scholte (ed.) *Building Global Democracy? Civil Society and Accountable Global Governance.* Cambridge: Cambridge University Press.

Searle, J. R. 2005. 'What is an Institution?' *Journal of Institutional Economics.* 1, 1: 1–22.

Simmons, B. A., and R. H. Steinberg (eds.). 2006. *International Law and International Relations.* Cambridge: Cambridge University Press.

Sinclair, T. J. (ed.). 2004. *Global Governance: Critical Concepts in Political Science.* London and New York: Routledge.

Sinclair, T. J. 2005. *The New Masters of Capital: American Bond Rating Agencies and the Politics of Creditworthiness.* Ithaca, NY, and London: Cornell University Press.

Slaughter, A.-M. 2004. *A New World Order.* Princeton, NJ: Princeton University Press.

Soederberg, S. 2006. *Global Governance in Question: Empire, Class and the New Common Sense in Managing North–South Relations.* Winnipeg, MN: Arbeiter Ring Publishing.

Stone, D. 1996. *Capturing the Political Imagination: Think Tanks and the Policy Process.* London: Routledge.

Stone, R. W. 2011. *Controlling Institutions: International Organizations and the Global Economy.* New York: Cambridge University Press.

Strange, S. 1994. *States and Markets.* 2nd edition. London: Pinter.

United Nations. Millennium Development Goals. www.un.org/millenniumgoals/. Date accessed 1 March 2012.

Van der Pijl, K. 1998. *Transnational Classes and International Relations.* London: Routledge.

Waltz, K. N. 1979. *Theory of International Politics.* New York: McGraw-Hill.

Weiss, T. G. 2012. *What's Wrong with the United Nations and How to Fix It?* 2nd edition. Cambridge: Polity Press.

Whitman, J. 2005. *The Limits of Global Governance.* London: Routledge.

Whitman, J. (ed.). 2009. *Palgrave Advances in Global Governance.* Basingstoke: Palgrave Macmillan.

Whitworth, S. 1994. *Feminism in International Relations: Towards a Political Economy of Gender in Interstate and Non-Governmental Institutions.* Basingstoke: Palgrave Macmillan.

Wilkinson, R. 2005a. 'Introduction: Concepts and Issues in Global Governance' in R. Wilkinson (ed.) *The Global Governance Reader.* London: Routledge.

Wilkinson, R. (ed.). 2005b. *The Global Governance Reader.* London: Routledge.

Wilkinson, R. 2006. *The WTO: Crisis and the Governance of Global Trade.* London: Routledge.

Williamson, J. 1994. 'In Search of a Manual for Technopols' in J. Williamson (ed.) *The Political Economy of Policy Reform.* Washington, DC: Institute for International Economics.

Woods, N. 1999. 'Good Governance in International Organizations'. *Global Governance.* 5, 1: 39–61.

Young, O. R. (ed.). 1997. *Global Governance: Drawing Insights from the Environmental Experience.* Cambridge, MA: MIT Press.

Index